designing

WITH

PHOTOS

Your all-in-one guide to
photographing like a professional
and then using your photos in
incredibly creative and artistic ways.

ALLISON TYLER JONES

DONNA SMYLIE

Designing With Photos is the fourth book in a series of books
published under the imprint "The Sophisticated Scrapbook," a
division of Autumn Leaves.

PUBLISHER: Autumn Leaves
BOOK DESIGN: Crystal Folgmann
COVER DESIGN: Crystal Folgmann and Donna Smylie
CREATIVE DIRECTION: Allison Tyler Jones and Donna Smylie
PHOTOGRAPHERS: Allison Tyler Jones and Donna Smylie
PRODUCT SAMPLE PHOTOGRAPHY: Tevis Photographic
WRITER: Allison Tyler Jones
EDITOR: Leta Baker

For information about bulk sales or
promotional pricing, please contact:
Josie Kinnear at Autumn Leaves
4917 Genesta Ave.
Encino, California 91316
1.800.588.6707
WWW.AUTUMNLEAVES.COM

ISBN 0-9714913-0-5

The Sophisticated Scrapbook
A Division of Autumn Leaves
Encino, California

Printed in the USA

Dedication

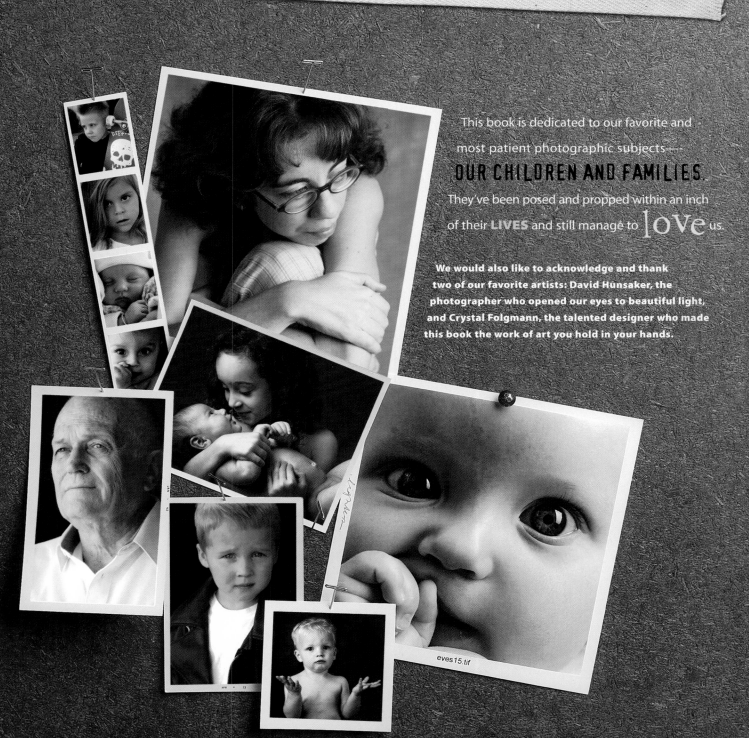

This book is dedicated to our favorite and most patient photographic subjects— **OUR CHILDREN AND FAMILIES.** They've been posed and propped within an inch of their **LIVES** and still manage to *love* us.

We would also like to acknowledge and thank two of our favorite artists: David Hunsaker, the photographer who opened our eyes to beautiful light, and Crystal Folgmann, the talented designer who made this book the work of art you hold in your hands.

eves15.tif

table of contents

WELCOME
to the files of our photographic experience.

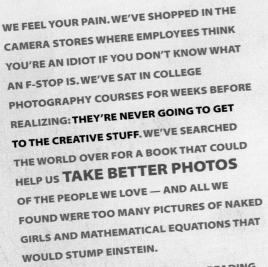

WE FEEL YOUR PAIN. WE'VE SHOPPED IN THE CAMERA STORES WHERE EMPLOYEES THINK YOU'RE AN IDIOT IF YOU DON'T KNOW WHAT AN F-STOP IS. WE'VE SAT IN COLLEGE PHOTOGRAPHY COURSES FOR WEEKS BEFORE REALIZING: **THEY'RE NEVER GOING TO GET TO THE CREATIVE STUFF.** WE'VE SEARCHED THE WORLD OVER FOR A BOOK THAT COULD HELP US **TAKE BETTER PHOTOS** OF THE PEOPLE WE LOVE — AND ALL WE FOUND WERE TOO MANY PICTURES OF NAKED GIRLS AND MATHEMATICAL EQUATIONS THAT WOULD STUMP EINSTEIN.

AFTER YEARS OF TAKING PHOTOS, READING EVERYTHING IN SIGHT AND FLYING CROSS-COUNTRY TO PHOTO WORKSHOPS, WE'RE CONVINCED THAT WE'VE NOT ONLY HEARD IT ALL, WE'VE BOUGHT IT ALL. WE'VE ENOUGH EXTRANEOUS EQUIPMENT BETWEEN US TO START A USED PHOTO EQUIPMENT STORE.

BUT OUR YEARS OF TRIAL AND ERROR (AND SOME SUCCESSES) NOW ALLOW US TO SHARE THE BENEFIT OF OUR EXPERIENCES. AND IF WE CAN LEARN TO TAKE DECENT PHOTOS, ANYONE CAN. WE'VE NOW BEEN TEACHING PHOTO WORKSHOPS AT OUR ARIZONA STORE FOR EIGHT YEARS. OUR BIGGEST THRILL WILL ALWAYS BE SEEING THAT LIGHT GO ON IN OUR STUDENTS' EYES AS THEY REALIZE: **PHOTOGRAPHY DOESN'T HAVE TO BE HARD.** THE CAMERA IS ONLY A TOOL. CREATIVITY CAN BE LEARNED AND **YOU CAN BE A GOOD PHOTOGRAPHER.**

This book is divided into two complete sections. The first is designed as a reference to help you take beautiful photos of those you love. The second offers entirely new ways to present and play with the amazing images you'll have soon created – to truly design with photos.

The inside covers of this book are an inspirational gallery of work from former students. These photos are proof positive that if you apply the simple assignments in each chapter, your photos will be better immediately, today, right now; no matter what camera you have and regardless of your experience.

SO IMMERSE YOURSELF IN OUR FILES AND TAKE YOUR FIRST STEPS ON A ROAD THAT IS ENDLESSLY CHALLENGING.

Best of Luck,

ALLISON + DONNA

THINK like a photographer

Learning to think like a photographer begins by SEEING the world in a whole new way. Instead of just looking at our surroundings, we must learn to really see them: light and shadow; form and line, expression and movement. These elements have always surrounded us, but as Sherlock Holmes said to Dr. Watson, "You observe, but you do not see."

In pondering this approach, consider the difference between the words:

DOCUMENTATION and INTERPRETATION

doc·u·ment (dăk′yə mənt; *for v.* -ment′) *n.* [ME. & OFr. < L. *documentum*, lesson, example, proof < *docere*, to teach: see DOCTOR] 1. anything printed, written, etc., relied upon to record or prove something 2. anything serving as proof —*vt.* 1. to provide with a document or documents 2. to provide (a book, pamphlet, etc.) with references as proof or support of things said 3. to prove or support, as by reference to documents —**doc′u·men′tal** (-men′t'l) *adj.*
doc·u...

in·ter·pret (in tʉr′prit; *...* < MFr. *interpréter* < L. *interpretari* < *interpres*, agent between two parties, broker, interpreter] 1. to explain the meaning of; make understandable [to *interpret* a poem] 2. to translate (esp. oral remarks) 3. to have or show one's own understanding of the meaning of; construe [to *interpret* a silence as contempt] 4. to bring out the meaning of; esp., to give one's own conception of (a work of art), as in performance —*vi.* to act as an interpreter; explain or trans... criticism... —SYN. see EXPLAIN —**in·ter**...

Documentation is a useful, **STRAIGHTFORWARD** way of recording **INFORMATION**. This photo says: "Alissa, 18 months." Documentation is a **SPECIFIC** person at a **SPECIFIC** place at a **SPECIFIC** time. It answers the simple questions: "Who, when and where?"

Interpretation asks as many questions as it answers. Interpretation **TELLS A STORY**. It's you seeing beyond the obvious, getting inside the picture and sharing your **FEELINGS** about a subject. Instead of "Alissa, 18 months," this photo says: "chunky toddler; spunky, soft, sweet and innocent."

"The best pictures, for me, are those which go straight into the heart and the blood, and take some time to reach the brain."

— Bill Jay

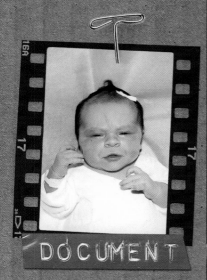

DOCUMENT

WHO? Alexandra

WHEN? At birth

WHERE? In the hospital

The first time I saw this baby girl, I felt overwhelmed by her beauty, innocence and tiny size. The mere presence of a newborn can inspire incredible feelings of tenderness — and renew our faith in infinite possibility.

INTERPRET

DELICATE
fresh
innocent
NEW

WHO? Sharon
WHEN? Delivery day
WHERE? At home

Sharon wanted to celebrate the pregnancy of her fourth and final child. I wanted to capture that perfectly pregnant belly and her intense love for this precious little one she had yet to meet.

INTERPRET

motherhood

ripe SACRIFICE
love succulent
NURTURE
round
full

CROP

8

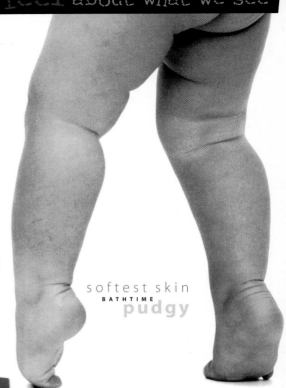

DOCUMENT

WHO? Keaton
WHEN? 3rd grade
WHERE? At school

I spent all afternoon trying to capture Keaton's vibrant nature and carefree attitude. After three rolls of film and nothing clicking, I packed up to leave. Just then, he jumped up on a tree stump for one last Tarzan yell.

softest skin
BATHTIME
pudgy

INTERPRET

spunky
BOY
carefree
freedom

Max may not be my baby, however, his cute little fanny still hangs on my living room wall. His chubby legs and toes say "every baby" to me, standing for those fleeting moments that fade far too quickly.

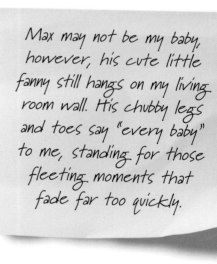

DOCUMENT

WHO? Max
WHEN? 7 months
WHERE? Studio

Instead of taking a typical family photo, why not think about it in terms of relationships? It doesn't have to be one big group. Try dividing everyone up and recording their spontaneous interactions. Your task is SIMPLY capturing the love between them.

RELATIONSHIPS

REMEMBER:
No amount of technical expertise can make up for lack of emotion in an image

emotion

connection

Learning to see is a photographer's single-most **IMPORTANT TOOL**. Fortunately, it's also a talent that can be learned and developed: the skill of acquiring a *critical eye*.

ASSIGNMENT

DEVELOP YOUR CRITICAL EYE

To work on your critical eye, try the following exercise.

Here's all you need:

- Several of your favorite magazines (our favorites include: *O*®*, The Oprah Magazine* , *Real Simple*®, *Victoria*®, *Vanity Fair*® and *Martha Stewart Living*®)

- A Post-it ® Note Pad

- A pen or pencil

Sift through the magazines and tear out or mark any photos that resonate with you. Ask yourself these questions about each photo:

- Do you feel an emotional connection (positive or negative) with this image?

- Does it relate anything about the human condition or our common experience?

- Does the photo say more to you than just who, what, when or where?

If the answer to two or more of these questions is yes, then you are looking at an interpretive photograph. Otherwise, it probably falls into the documentation category. Why not start collecting your favorite images right now?

2 TOOLBOX

The first thing that comes to mind after gazing at a masterpiece painting is probably not, **"I bet Van Gogh used really good brushes."** Why then, when you take a really nice photo, do people say, **"YOU MUST HAVE A REALLY GOOD CAMERA?"**

A camera and all its accessories are just TOOLS. Granted, some tools are better than others. Some give you more options to work with, but in the end, these tools do only what we make them do. The VISION is within the photographer ALONE.

The truth is, we too often use our tools without thinking. You feel like you have "the shot" but what you get back looks nothing like your original vision. Understanding a few essential camera functions will give you CONFIDENCE — CONFIDENCE that you can get the shot, and CONFIDENCE that you can repeat those masterpiece-quality results.

Basic Camera Types
FILM OR DIGITAL

POINT-AND-SHOOT

— Compact and lightweight

— Easy to learn and use

— Best for trips and snapshots

— Auto-everything gives you less creative control

— What you see through the viewfinder IS NOT necessarily what you get

— Lenses are not interchangeable

SINGLE-LENS REFLEX (SLR)

— Can be bulky and heavy (depending on the lens)

— Steeper learning curve

— Best for portraits and fine-art photography

— Auto- or manual-exposure modes give you more creative control

— What you see through the viewfinder IS INDEED what you get

— Interchangeable lenses

the BIG three

Ready to eliminate those out-of-focus, over-flashed photos from your life? To do so, there are **three main functions** you must be able to control on your camera.

Before

After

1 AUTO-FOCUS LOCK

Not to be confused with auto exposure, auto-focus lock lets you lock focus on your subject and then reframe your shot, keeping your subject in focus. We've all seen photos of two people where the background looks great but the actual subjects are out of focus. Auto focus helps prevent this — and also lets you photograph a subject off-center. (see below)

DO IT

For a two-person shot, place the little center mark in your viewfinder on one person. Press the shutter-release button halfway down, then, while keeping the button pressed halfway down, reframe your shot to include both subjects and take the picture. **NOTE:** When photographing two people, both must be the same distance from the camera or one will be out of focus. This method also works well when you don't want your subject front and center.

Before Focus Lock

After

Off-Center Subject

2 MINIMUM FOCUSING DISTANCE

Your minimum focusing distance is the closest distance you can get to your subject and still maintain focus. An auto-focus SLR camera will resist taking a photo if it's not in focus, so you may hear a whirring focusing motor and have difficulty taking your shot. Point-and-shoot cameras are a little trickier. Because the viewfinder doesn't show you exactly what the lens is seeing, the picture can look fine to you while taking it but still come out blurry because you were too close. Most point-and-shoot cameras have a minimum focusing distance of 3-4 feet.

DO IT

Use your arm as a reference when getting close to a subject. Most arms are about 3 feet long, so allow an arm's distance and then some to be safe. That's as close as you can physically get and still maintain focus. If this isn't close enough for you to get the shot you want, stay back 3-4 feet but use the zoom function to get closer. Your limit is being both as physically close and zoomed in as possible. If it's still not close enough, you may need a different lens — or even a different camera.

3 FLASH CONTROL

In order to use your flash to correct bad lighting or avoid any flash at all you must be able to control your flash settings. This requires simply reading your camera's manual to learn how to keep your flash off when it wants to be on, and on when it wants to be off.

DO IT

Consult your manual to determine which flash functions your camera has. The buttons or settings to look for are "fill flash" or "flash on" for flash on every shot or "flash off" for no flash at all.

Before

After

13

Photographer's Note:
Don't try to save money by buying a cheap lens — you'll regret it. A lens has more impact on your pictures than any other piece of equipment, so invest wisely.

A good camera bag with adjustable sections you can configure for your equipment.

A tripod for holding your camera VERY still.

A small notebook for making creative notes about an upcoming photo shoot (about your subjects, the setup, wardrobe, etc.).

A point-and-shoot, auto-everything camera for vacations and times when you don't want to lug the big camera around.

A mid-range zoom lens 35-135mm (the human eye sees at approximately 50mm). Less than 50mm is considered wide angle and more than 50mm is considered telephoto. A 35-135mm lens gives you the best of all worlds.

As far as equipment goes, you need surprisingly little to get started. When we began photography as a hobby, we purchased so many things we didn't need. After years of experience, we've streamlined our equipment to include the following items.

our TOOL kit

WHICH CAMERA SHOULD I BUY?

Stick with the major brands. Donna uses Canon equipment and Allison prefers Nikon. Both companies have excellent quality and their equipment is similarly priced.

HAND-HELD TEST

After determining your budget and the functions you require, take the hand-held test. Hold the camera in your hands. Does it feel good? Can you get a feeling for how to use it without getting out the manual immediately? If all things are equal but one model just feels better than the other, then buy the one that feels best.

A good camera strap. But don't wear it around your neck. Wrap it a couple of times around your wrist EVERY time you pick up your camera. If you make it a habit, you'll never drop your camera.

A 35mm SLR camera (film and/or digital) with the following features:

AUTO FOCUS
Auto focus allows your lens to automatically focus wherever you point it. It's perfect for capturing fast-moving subjects, like toddlers, and absolutely essential if your eyesight isn't what it used to be.

AUTO AND MANUAL EXPOSURE
If you're going to pursue photography as a hobby, it's important to be able to use your camera in manual mode as well as program or automatic mode. This gives you the flexibility to compensate for tricky lighting situations or take advantage of a creative opportunity.

Backup batteries, film and/or digital media cards.

A UV filter that screws onto the end of the lens to protect it from scratches and dust.

Photographer's Note:
If you're not sure about a piece of equipment, rent it first. Most equipment can be rented over a weekend for a nominal fee. It's well worth it to prevent a bad purchase.

EXPOSURE

For any given photo, the right exposure lets in **JUST** the amount of light to make that picture perfect — not too dark and not too light. The only way to take a properly exposed picture is by controlling the amount of light reaching your film or digital processor. You do this by either **CONTROLLING THE APERTURE** or the SHUTTER SPEED to dramatically affect the look of your photos.

Aperture

NOTE: Control over depth of field is PURELY for creative effect; so don't get too hung up on the technical side of it. You just need to learn enough to achieve the results you want.

The aperture is the opening that allows light through your lens. The numbers that measure the size of the opening are called f-stops. Here's where it gets a little confusing. The larger the f-stop number, the smaller the opening (f16 is smaller than f8). The opposite is true, too: the smaller the f-stop number, the larger the opening (f2.8 is larger than f5.6). Who thought this up, anyway? The easiest way to make sense of it all is to think of the numbers as fractions: 1/16 is obviously smaller than 1/8. Thinking about squinting also helps. When you can't see something very well, you squint to try and see it better. This is the eye's way of "closing down" the aperture to get more of "the picture" into focus.

The **MAIN THING** the aperture setting controls is the depth of field, which is essentially the amount of the picture that's in or out of focus. If most of your photo (the foreground, middle ground and background) is all in focus, then it has a long depth of field. The photo of a father and son has a long depth of field

Long Depth of Field

Short Depth of Field

because, even though the dad stands a distance behind his son, they're both in focus. If just a little bit of your photo is in focus, then it has a short depth of field. The same photo of father and son with a short depth of field yields dramatically different results.

Very Short Depth of Field

Sometimes the depth of field is so shallow that one eye of your subject can be in focus while the other is not. This usually happens when you are shooting "wide open," or at the widest possible aperture (in this case 2.8).

It helps to **PREVISUALIZE** what you'd like your end results to be. Do you want part of the photo sharp and part out of focus? Or do you want the whole photo sharp, foreground to background? It seems logical to want everything in perfect focus all the time,

right? Why would anyone want blurry photos? Flip through the photos you've been clipping out of magazines and you'll quickly see why a little blur now and then is a very good thing.

If you've got a distracting background, throw it out of focus by using a short depth of field.

Maybe you're shooting a gorgeous landscape or monument on a trip and you want everything inch of it perfect focus.

Long Depth of Field

Long Depth of Field

Short Depth of Field

Remember
LARGE APERTURE
= **LESS** of your photo will be sharp
SMALL APERTURE
= **MORE** of your photo will be sharp

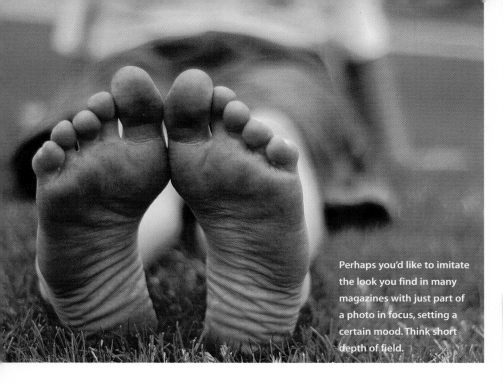

Perhaps you'd like to imitate the look you find in many magazines with just part of a photo in focus, setting a certain mood. Think short depth of field.

Shutter Speed

Shutter speed is the amount of **time** the shutter remains open once you take your photo. Moving subjects can be shown sharp and frozen or blurred to varying degrees. A fast shutter speed like 1/500 freezes motion while a slow shutter speed like 1/30 shows movement or blur.

Fast Shutter Speed

Slow Shutter Speed

EXPOSURE MODES

YOUR CAMERA MAY HAVE SOME OR ALL OF THESE SETTINGS. LEARN WHAT THEY CAN DO AND GET MORE CONTROL OVER YOUR PHOTOGRAPHY.

EXPOSURE MODE	WHAT IT DOES
FULLY AUTOMATIC	Your camera makes all the decisions
PREPROGRAMMED MODES *(Usually denoted by icons)*	
Face Profile = portrait mode	Short depth of field to blur background
Runner = sports mode	Fast shutter speed to freeze action
Mountain = landscape mode	Long depth of field for landscapes
Flower = close-up mode	Short depth of field and macro lens setting for extreme closeups
PRIORITY MODES	
Shutter priority	You set the shutter speed, the camera sets the aperture (Great for when you want to freeze a moving subject)
Aperture priority	You set the aperture, the camera sets the shutter speed (The mode you use most to control depth of field)
FULLY MANUAL	You set everything, both the aperture and shutter speed

ASSIGNMENT

Consult your manual to see which exposure modes your camera has (see table). Shoot the same photo in all the different modes and see what you come up with. Keep notes so that you know which exposure was taken in what mode. **COMPARE YOUR RESULTS.**

the DIGITAL difference

The big question on everyone's mind is: FILM or DIGITAL? Our answer is yes. Actually, both film and digital cameras were used to create the images in this book.

The main thing to consider before going digital is that digital cameras are just one small part of a larger digital system. To truly take advantage of all a digital camera has t o offer, you also need a computer with a CD burner and photo-editing software to manipulate your images once you've captured them.

DIGITAL dynamics

INSTANT GRATIFICATION

What you see IS what you get — and you get to see it immediately. You benefit by becoming a better photographer far faster because you're working with instant results. No more lost rolls of film due to accidentally adjusting your camera's setting incorrectly.

Digital cameras tend to be more expensive than their film counterparts. And digital media (the little cards that record your images) may initially be more expensive than a roll of film, but you can use one card over and over. And though you save big on film and processing costs, by the time you buy a printer, ink cartridges and photo paper, you're just about even with film cameras.

WHICH DIGITAL CAMERA TO BUY?

Decide what you're willing to pay and find out how many mega pixels you can get for that amount (the more mega pixels, the better the image quality), then take the hand-held test and go with your gut.

IMAGE QUALITY

With digital cameras, there's a trade-off between image compression and image quality. Higher-quality images use less compression (sometimes called fine mode) and are ideal for larger prints. But since these images take up more memory space, you get fewer shots per card. With more compression (in normal or basic mode), you can store more images on your card, but these are best suited for smaller prints, Web sites or e-mail attachments.

WHITE BALANCE

All light is not the same. For example, indoor light bulbs give off warm light, while open-shade light provides cool light and fluorescent lighting has a greenish cast. In traditional photography, you would use specific films or filters to compensate for different light temperatures. With a digital camera, you use the "white balance" setting. Many cameras now have pre-programmed settings for indoor, outdoor or fluorescent lighting, etc. Some may allow you to manually set a white balance while pointing the camera at a white card or surface. Other cameras have automatic white balance.

> **NOTE:** Film images can also be scanned into a digital format, allowing you to take advantage of all the digital benefits.

IMAGE SIZE — DO THE MATH

Decide what size you want your final image to be. If you're not sure, it's probably safer to shoot a little larger than necessary. You can always reduce the size from there, whereas you can't increase it later if you start out too small.

Here's a handy chart to help you decide on an image size. Start with your desired final print size on the left, and then move right to see what size of file you'll need.

Quality/ppi* Print Size	FINE/300PPI Pixel Size	File Size	NORMAL/150PPI Pixel Size	File Size	BASIC/80PPI Pixel Size	File Size
4x6	1200x1800	738KB	600x900	44KB	320x480	34KB
5x7	1500x2100	963KB	750x1050	57KB	400x560	45KB
8x10	2400x3000	2.16MB	1200x1500	114KB	640x800	85KB

*Pixels per inch
**Saved in a JPEG Format

SHUTTER DELAY

With film cameras, it's SNAP — and you've got the shot. With many digital cameras, there's a delay between you pressing the shutter button and the picture being taken. Think of a digital camera as a digital scanner with a lens. It makes sense why it would take a little longer to record each photo. The exact length of this delay is also a factor in the cost of the camera. Digital point-and-shoot cameras tend to have longer delays than the more expensive digital SLRs that allow you to shoot 5-6 photos in a row with no delay at all.

LOADING SPEED

If you're shooting at a very high resolution, like with fine mode, it may take up to 30 seconds for an image to load onto your digital card. Meanwhile, you can't take any more photos until loading is complete. As with all digital equipment, from computers to cameras, speed costs money — the faster a camera takes and loads pictures, the more it costs.

PLAYBACK BONUS

Since digital cameras let you play back images immediately, you can delete any unwanted shots right away, leaving more room on your card for better photos. **BEWARE:** Images that look perfectly in focus on a tiny LCD screen can actually be soft and blurry when enlarged. Review the Big Three to perfect your focusing techniques.

OUTPUT OPTIONS

There are so many things you can do with digital pictures:

- E-mail to family and friends
- Drop into a word-processing document
- Upload to an Internet service for printing on T-shirts, stationery, etc.
- Upload to an Internet service for traditional prints and enlargements
- Burn to a CD and take to a local photo processor for traditional prints and enlargements
- Store and print out on your home computer
- Manipulate the image in a software program (like Adobe® Photoshop®)

3 FILM file

Choosing film according to the light available and the possible movement of your subject will give you the confidence that what you see IS what you'll get.

When taking pictures, **WHAT YOU SEE** isn't **ALWAYS WHAT YOU GET**. And that has a lot to do with **THE FILM** you select for each subject. you see your daughter in the middle of her first dance recital. YOU GET a blurry mass of bodies. you see your kids fast asleep in each other's arms. YOU GET a distracting orange glow around their faces. you see your son sitting on Dad's lap. YOU GET a too dark, could've-been-perfect portrait.

NOTE: Even the slight movement of your camera can cause blurry shots in low light.

Why such a big difference between what we originally see and what we actually get? Film is simply not as sophisticated as the human eye. While we see in a broad spectrum of color, light and shadow, each film type is only sensitive to specific parts of that spectrum. That's why there are so many different types of film on the market.

Among your options, slow-speed film (100 and 200) requires the most light and time to record an image. Medium- to fast-speed film (400, 800 and even 1600) needs much less light and time to capture the same shot.

Believe it or not, choosing the right film speed is actually pretty easy.

THE TWO MAIN FACTORS TO CONSIDER ARE:

The amount of light that will be available while shooting. Will it be: Noon or evening? Indoors or outside? Sunny or overcast?

Whether your subject(s) will be standing still or moving around. A strutting puppy needs faster film than Grandma sitting and knitting.

FILM FILM FILM FILM FILM FILM

SLOW-SPEED FILMS

If you're headed to the beach and it's a sunny day, you'd better find some 100- or 200-speed film — anything else will be too fast, potentially causing pictures to come out grainy in appearance.

MEDIUM-SPEED FILMS

Your best all-around film is 400-speed. It works well outdoors (as long as light is not too bright) and it's nice for window portraits (as long as it's not too dark).

FAST-SPEED FILMS

For shooting on an overcast day or capturing fast-moving subjects like players in an afternoon ballgame, use 800-speed film.

When you're photographing indoor sporting events from too high up in the bleachers to use flash, or taking candlelight shots of kids and birthday cakes or other interior moments where flash isn't an option, spring or 1600-speed* film.

*If you use a point-and-shoot camera, check your manual before investing in film of this high a speed (to make sure it's compatible).

Once you've committed to a film speed, don't be shy.

SHOOT THE whole roll.

If you're one of those people who keep one roll of film in their camera for six months and expect that film to capture it all — it's time for a little  REALITY

Digital Note:

1 When in doubt, use a faster speed than you think you'll need.

2 Digital cameras require you to set the film speed using ISO control. Use the information above for help in selecting your digital ISO setting.

MAKE A PROMISE TO YOURSELF WHEN LOADING YOUR CAMERA WITH FILM:

A promise to use at least one WHOLE ROLL at each event.
— One whole roll at that out-of-control birthday party.
— One whole roll of your family playing on the beach.
— One whole roll as your baby practices crawling.

COLOR or Black & White?

THE PROS

Color represents images as real life, which makes it perfect for taking snapshots or documenting an event.

When the colors of your subject are integral to telling its story, like during a trip to Disneyland or attending a costume party, color film is a no-brainer.

Color film is forgiving. Because we see in color, mistakes in composition and lighting aren't so obvious.

Color works well for environmental portraits, like a child in his room or Grandpa at his workbench.

THE CONS

Color can be distracting. Complexion-challenged teenagers and ruddy newborns, for example, look better in black and white.

Virtually all color film sold for amateur use is color-balanced for daylight and offers best results in daylight or with flash. This can be a problem when shooting indoors. Fluorescent light tends to show up greenish and incandescent light casts a warm, yellowish-orange color on pictures.

Natural Light

Incandescent Light

Flourescent Light

WHY BLACK & WHITE?

THE PROS

There's nothing like a beautiful black-and-white print to make you feel like you've created art.

Black and white is great for portraits. The tones and textures are flattering to just about anyone. Plus, it tends to make people look skinnier (and we're all for that!).

Black and white is ideal for newborns and subjects with red undertones to their skin. See the difference in this photo of Cole and Will. The color photo has "snapshot" written all over it while the black-and-white version serves as a timeless portrait of new brothers.

Black and white reduces an image to its very essence.

THE CONS

Line and texture are more dominant in black and white, so you have to pay more attention to clothing patterns and backgrounds.

Contrast can make or break an image. A muddy print with no real blacks or whites isn't pleasing to look at. Colors that may have given you great contrast with color film don't necessarily work in black and white. With color film, red and blue look very different; but in black and white, they register as virtually the same tone.

NOTE: You can pre-visualize your shot in black and white by squinting your eyes until all you see is tone and shape. Distracting areas will jump out at you, allowing you to recompose the photo or eliminate distractions.

Okay, so we admit it:

we have a serious bias toward black and white. And unless we're just taking snapshots, we rarely shoot with anything else.

ALLISON'S
Favorites

There's always a roll of **KODAK BLACK AND WHITE PLUS® 400** film in my camera bag. A C-41 film, labs can process it using color photochemistry, which means black-and-white prints in an hour. Black and White Plus® is almost impossible to mess up and it makes beautiful enlargements with very little grain.

When I want to be in control, start to finish (which means developing my own negatives and printing my own prints), I use **ILFORD FP4® 125**. It has gorgeous tones and very little grain. I only use it when I use my studio lights, as it tends to be too slow for most available lighting.

If I absolutely have to shoot in color, I prefer **KODAK'S PORTRA 400 NC®**. This is a professional film only found in pro labs or camera shops. Portra renders beautiful skin tones that you can almost feel.

ALLISON SAYS

Find a Film You Like and Learn It.

When I first got into photography, I bought every kind of film and drove myself crazy trying to figure each one out. I now realize that when all is said and done, it's what's ON the film that counts the most. The type of film you use is simply a tool for getting results. Luckily, this is one area where we've done a lot of work for you.

Favorites

KODAK TMAX 3200 is an extremely fast film. Perfect for situations where there is very little available light. I took this window-light portrait of Hailee and her harp on an overcast winter day. The 3200-speed film allowed me to capture her movement while playing the harp. The fast speed of the film also makes it super-grainy which gives the image an almost impressionistic feel.

Kodak Professional
T-MAX P3200 FILM
P3200 TMAX
BLACK & WHITE NEGATIVE FILM
FILM NÉGATIF NOIR ET BLANC
135-36   P3200TMZ

KODAK PORTRA® 400 NC is a film offering accurate, natural color. The centuries-old bedroom pictured was in a French village. I was determined to capture its pale, washed-out feeling. A vivid color film wouldn't have worked. As this was a still-life picture, movement wasn't an issue, so I placed my camera on a chair and used a slow shutter speed to record the image.

DONNA SAYS

Keep It Simple.

Use one film, one subject and one lighting setup for a single photo shoot. Limiting variables makes it easier to learn and to reproduce a look you like in the future.

KODAK BLACK AND WHITE PLUS® 400 is my first choice for most photos. It can be developed at a one-hour processing lab and is very forgiving of imperfect lighting situations. This allows even amateur photographers to get great shots.

4 the PRINT

The average person takes snapshots — a few frames of this, a few frames of that. The prints are the end of the road, serving as photos to be stored in an album or a frame.

A photographer works with **proofs**, taking lots of shots per subject and then using the resulting prints (or proofs) to **DETERMINE WHICH SHOTS ARE BEST**. Proofing can be done with either film or digital images.

"Good photograps are seen in the mind's eye before the shutter is tripped."

— Anonymous

PROOFS

HERE ARE SOME WAYS TO PROOF (OR PRE-PROOF) WITH DIGITAL IMAGES:

- Pre-proof images in your camera during a photo shoot.

- Pre-proof images on your computer screen after the shoot.

- If you prefer proofing actual prints, we've found it's most satisfying to have them printed on real photographic paper by a photo processor. Most one-hour labs and warehouse merchants offer one-hour print services for digital images.

PHOTOGRAPHER'S NOTE: We have our film or digital images processed at a one-hour lab. It's a fast way to get proofs back so you can start making decisions. The 4"x 6" prints make it easy to show crop marks and printing instructions for a custom lab to follow.

CROPPING

IN-CAMERA CROPPING

After years of photographing people, we find it easier to crop an image while shooting it. There'll be times when you need to crop your images after you've taken the photos, but in-camera cropping not only saves you time, it makes you a better photographer. Stop yourself from thinking "I can do that part later" and give in-camera cropping a try. Frame the same shot both wide and zoomed-in to get more choices in your final print.

Sometimes you get a so-so shot that becomes fabulous with a little cropping.

CROPPING TOOLS

Cropping "Ls" are essential tools for cropping your photos. Here's how to get them: cut two L-shapes out of cardstock and use them to frame opposite corners, moving them around to find the perfect crop. Then use a permanent marker or grease pencil to mark your proofs. A custom lab will use these marks as a guide when creating your final print. An added benefit of using L-shapes to crop your proofs is that your in-camera cropping skills will naturally improve. Just the act of looking at the same photo in a variety of crops increases your ability to frame a shot any time.

CUSTOM Lab services

Custom labs (or professional labs) provide services that you just can't get from most one-hour labs. And you don't have to be a professional to take advantage of the expertise available there. The services we use most include:

AFTER

CUSTOM ENLARGEMENTS

While one-hour labs can usually print enlargements up to 8"x 10" size, a custom lab can go even bigger — way bigger (we recently had a photo printed 10 feet by 10 feet). A pro lab can also custom print your photo. Custom printing involves making sure color is balanced (important for digital images) and exposure is correct, along with lightening or darkening selected areas of the image that need it.

GOING FROM COLOR TO BLACK AND WHITE

Did you know that color film negatives can be turned into black-and-white prints? This is a revelation to many of our students, and a fun experiment to try. It works especially well for those bad-color photos we all have from the 70s.

CREATING CONTACT PRINTS

Mentioned previously as a way to proof your shots, these mini photos are so cute and fun to use. You can have a contact print made from any set of negatives.

CREATIVE CROPPING

As with most photographic successes, this one started out as a mistake. A black background confused a lab's machinery and this was the result. Amazing how an extreme crop can take a so-so shot and make it into something interesting. Just ask a lab to print your negative in panoramic mode.

CUSTOM B/W PRINTS

If you shoot Kodak Black and White Plus® film, your proofs may come back with a slight color shift. Instead of true black and white, they might have a blue or sepia tone to them. This is because, although this film is a black and white film, it is developed in color chemistry (known as C-41) and the one-hour labs print it onto color paper. To get true black-and-white prints, select from your proofs and have your enlargements made on true black-and-white photographic paper at a custom lab.

BEFORE

NOTE: Custom Labs also let you choose which type of paper you'd like your photo printed on. Glossy or matte, anyone?

ASSIGNMENT

#1

1 Look up Photography in your yellow pages. Find a custom photo lab near you.

2 Find the negative or digital file for a photo that makes you particularly proud.

3 Go to the lab and have an 8"x 10" (or larger) print made.

4 Consider this your first portfolio piece.

ASSIGNMENT

#2

1 Find a proof (print) and use your L-shapes to mark it for cropping. Also mark any areas you'd like to see lighter or darker. Take both the print and the negative to the lab.

2 For a digital file, you can crop the image in your photo manipulation software (i.e. Adobe® Photoshop®). Make your crop then go to the lab.

3 Have an enlargement made.

ASSIGNMENT

#3

1 Find the negative for a color print you'd like to see in black and white.

2 Take it to the lab and ask them to print it in black and white. It's that simple.

3 If you have a digital file, convert a color image to black and white using software.

5 get CLOSER

What's the subject of this photo?

Is it a sidewalk or a lamppost?

Wait — is that a child on a bike?

Could she be the intended subject?

The photographer wanted a picture of a little girl on her bicycle. What he got was a picture with no clear subject.

Sound familiar? That's because the single most **COMMON MISTAKE** new photographers make is not getting close enough to their subjects. The more you photograph, the more you'll realize that what you see isn't always what you get.

Photographer's Note:
Remind yourself to always check the four corners of your viewfinder for distracting elements BEFORE you shoot — you'll be amazed at the difference in your photos.

"If your pictures aren't good enough, you're not close enough."

—Robert Capa,

Photojournalist

you see
Your daughter playing with the family pooch in the backyard.

you get ☛
A shot that includes plenty of dirt, weeds and a block wall.

By simply **GETTING CLOSER** you can emphasize your subject and eliminate distractions.

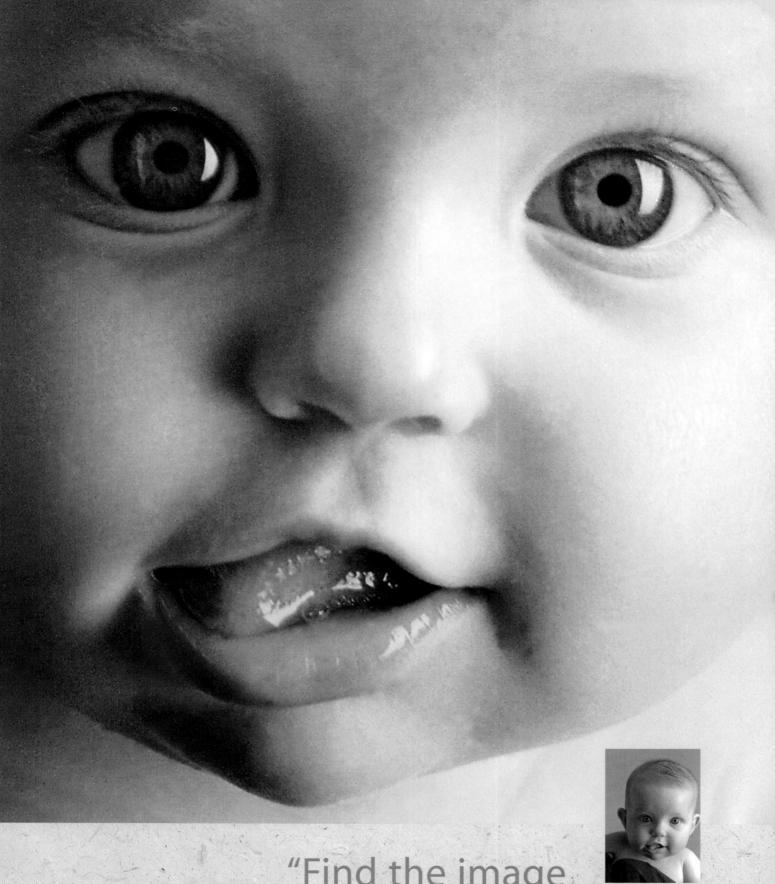

"Find the image
within the image."

— DAVE TEVIS

Getting up-close and personal with your subject does two very important things:

- It simplifies your image.
- It emphasizes your subject.

really CLOSE...

TO GET CLOSER YOU HAVE TO MOVE IT.

MOVE YOUR subject — BRING IT CLOSER TO YOU.

MOVE yourself — GET CLOSER TO YOUR SUBJECT.

MOVE YOUR camera — ZOOM IN WITH YOUR LENS.

even CLOSER...

THINK OF YOUR SUBJECT IN PIECES. You can create more abstract images by moving in really close.

abstracts

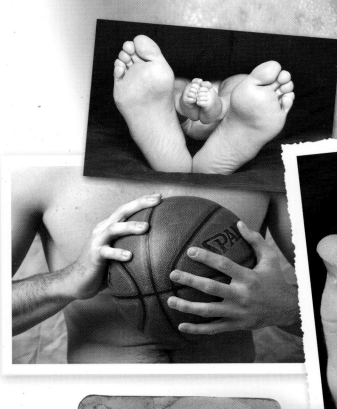

ASSIGNMENT

1 Determine the minimum focusing distance for your camera or lens (see Chapter 2 for details).

2 Shoot an entire roll of film with one goal: Getting Closer.

3 Before taking each shot, check the four corners of your viewfinder for any distracting elements and then reframe the shot if necessary.

4 In addition to framing your subject more closely, try a few abstract shots. To do so, photograph your subject in pieces, perhaps just focusing on the toes, hands or eyes.

Photographer's Note:

For great close-ups, get as PHYSICALLY close as you can (remembering your camera's minimum focusing distance) and then use your lens to zoom in further.

6 LET there be LIGHT

Before you even pick up a camera, walk around your home or neighborhood and **TAKE IN** the light. See how it changes at different times of day. **PAY CLOSE ATTENTION** to how it falls on your baby's face while he sleeps. Observe how light and shadow work together to create form and texture on objects around you. The ability to see light isn't learned in a day. Mastering the art of lighting is a photographer's lifelong pursuit.

Begin your journey of observation today.

"Come into the light of things. Let nature be your teacher."

– William Wordsworth

LIGHT
is all around us.

It comes through the bedroom window early in the morning. It dances in a child's caramel curls. It bathes the world in warm, golden tones just before day turns into evening. This play of light and shadow has inspired artists for centuries. **Let it inspire your photography.** We write with light every time we take a photo, though obviously some results are better than others. Some photos are too light, some too dark and every now and then we get a really amazing fluke of a shot. How does this happen? To create truly beautiful "light writings," you must first learn to SEE THE LIGHT.

The word photograph actually comes from two Greek words:

PHOTO = LIGHT
GRAPH = TO WRITE

To photograph is literally to write with light.

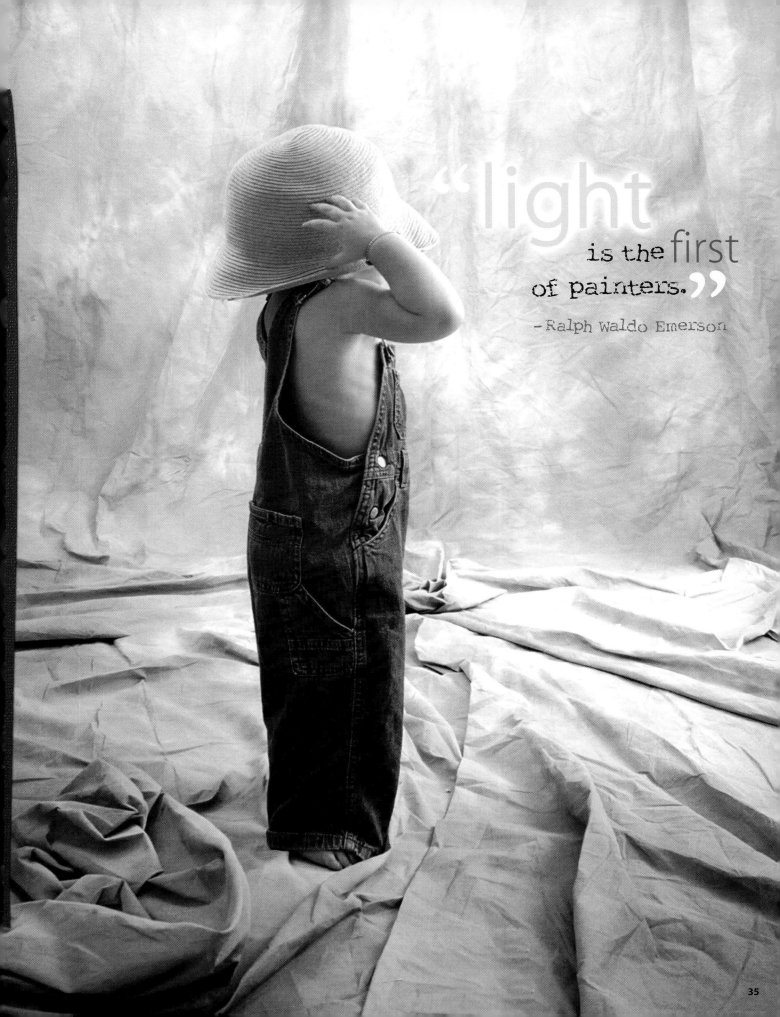

"light is the first of painters."

–Ralph Waldo Emerson

When shooting the average snapshot, we tend to worry more about getting enough light than we do about the quality of light we're seeing.

QUANTITY of light is important, but quality of light is what matters most.

HARD LIGHT

Hard light comes directly from the source. Sunlight and on-camera flash are two very direct forms of hard light. An easy way to determine hard light is noticing the hard line between light and shadow, hard enough that it looks like you could cut it out with scissors. When used improperly, hard light flattens a subject, eliminates details and produces harsh, unflattering shadows.

SOFT LIGHT

Soft light does not come directly from the source. Soft light is indirect, like sunlight filtering through curtains or diffused by clouds. With soft light, the line between light and shadow is less harsh than with direct light, and generally more suitable for photographing people.

EXCEPTION: If you see Elvis at Burger King®, you might be justified in using flash. Otherwise, keep it turned off.

Flash Is Evil

On-camera flash is the culprit in many photographic disasters. The over-flashed skin, demon-red eyes and harsh shadows all combine into a photographic nightmare. Flash can be like using the headlights of your car to illuminate an image. It gets the job done, but often with neither pretty nor flattering results.

Instead of turning on the flash, try using faster film or moving your subject to a better-lit location. The only reason to use on-camera flash is if there is NO OTHER WAY to get the shot (or if you're using it as fill-flash).

Modifying Light

It would be nice if great light could always be there when you needed it. Since that's not going to happen, it's helpful to know a few things about modifying the available light.

PROBLEM:
HARD, DIRECT LIGHT

SOLUTION:
DIFFUSE IT

When the available light is too harsh, try diffusing it. A diffuser can be a white curtain or sheet draped across a sunny window or a light-diffuser disk held by an assistant. Placed between the harsh light and the subject, diffusers even out the light for a better portrait.

PROBLEM:
NOT ENOUGH
LIGHT/DARK SHADOWS

SOLUTION:
REFLECT IT

When you need more light or when the shadows are too dark on one side of your subject, try a reflector. You can purchase a professional reflector at your local camera store or you can use reflectors found in your environment. A big piece of white foam core also makes a great reflector. Notice the sunlight reflecting off the wall on the left side of this portrait.

PROBLEM:
BACKLIGHT

SOLUTION:
MOVE IT

When the area behind your subject is much brighter than the actual subject, you have backlight. Snow, sunny skies or bright windows are all backlighting culprits. Solving this problem requires that you move either yourself or your subject.

1 Move or zoom in really closely on your subject so that it fills most of the frame.

2 Move your subject to a different angle from the light.

PROBLEM:
BACKLIGHT

SOLUTION:
FILL-FLASH IT

Fill-flash is another way to "clean up" distracting shadows in a photo if diffusion isn't an option. Fill-flash works great when shooting photos on the beach in bright, overhead sun or if you're photographing someone in a cap or visor and want their eyes to show up. Turn your flash to the fill-flash setting (assuming you have one). If not, just turn on your flash (check your manual if you have questions).

Finding the Light

Every room in your house becomes a potential photo studio when you learn to see light.

THE GARAGE

Garages have all the ingredients necessary for a successful photo shoot: lots of room and a big light source (the open door). Set up a background and invite the neighbor kids over for a posing contest.

WINDOWS

Nothing beats windows for gorgeous light. Note how close the couple is to the window. Set them up and shoot away.

PORCHES OR OPEN SHADE

The soft, flat lighting created by a porch overhang is perfect for almost any subject. Face them toward the light for the most flattering result.

THE BATH TUB

TIP: Tubs are also great places to contain a wild toddler for a minute while you snap a few shots.

Photographer's Note:

This photo of Dad and baby was taken in collaboration with Donna, Allison and photographer Elizabeth Opalenik. Elizabeth walked through Allison's house and found a spot to shoot in almost every room. Surprisingly, her favorite spot of all was the bath tub. The bath tub sits beneath a large glass-block window. The surrounding walls are painted white and since it's a relatively small area, the walls act as reflectors, providing gorgeous lighting. Put some comfy pillows in the bottom of the tub and your subject can relax while you shoot away!

Direction of Light

The direction from which the light hits your subject has significant impact on the look of your photo.

FLAT LIGHTING

Flat lighting tends to be frontal lighting. Flat lighting is achieved by having the subject face a diffused light source that eliminates shadows. When you're just getting started, flat lighting is an easy way to get good results. It's particularly nice because it naturally conceals blemishes and wrinkles.

3-D LIGHTING OR "REMBRANDT LIGHTING"

Although photography is two-dimensional, the proper use of light and shadow can lend your images a three-dimensional look. Artists have been doing it for centuries with paint; you can do it with a camera.

Rembrandt lighting is achieved by putting your subject at a 45- to 90-degree angle to a light source. The quality of light can be either hard or soft.

The grandfather and grandson (left) were photographed with an example of hard, direct light from a 45-degree angle. It's particularly effective with masculine subjects. The hard light shows the rugged detail in this grandpa's hands and neck, creating a nice contrast to the soft skin of his grandson.

The photo of this beautiful grandmother was taken with soft, indirect light at a 90-degree angle. The play of light and shadow over her face shows every bit of character and texture, but the softer light lends a more feminine feeling.

ASSIGNMENT

PAY ATTENTION TO THE LIGHT

Look through your idea file (refer to Chapter 1). Notice the different lighting styles and angles in each of the photos you've collected. To determine how a photo was lit, look at the reflections in the eyes of the subject(s). You'll be able to tell the angle of the light and whether or not they used a reflector. Look closely enough and you might even see the photographer's reflection.

As you're driving or walking, **PAY ATTENTION** to the light.

Watch the shadows at different times of day and start learning to identify types and angles of light.

RENT A MOVIE

Two movies with gorgeous **LIGHTING** are:

- *Meet Joe Black*, starring Brad Pitt and Anthony Hopkins

- *The House of Mirth*, starring Gillian Anderson

Start paying attention to lighting in all the movies you watch.

Check out the windows and doorways in your home. Is there one that has beautiful light at certain times of day? Artists have always favored north-facing windows because the light is indirect all year round. Do you have a north-facing window?

BOTTOM LINE:

MATCH the lighting to your subject.

The PHOTO SHOOT

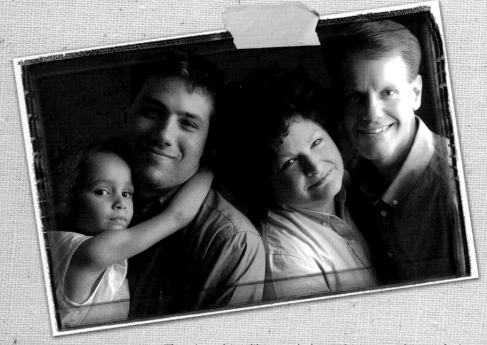

Those boy scouts had it right all along: **BE PREPARED.** The first thing you need to do to prepare for your photo shoot is answer a few questions that will help you make decisions during set up:

1 **Who will you be photographing?**
While you can photograph one person in a relatively small space, a group of people requires a much larger area.

2 **If it's more than one person, what is their relationship?**
Husband and wife, siblings, friends, parent and child —each of these **RELATIONSHIPS** can be portrayed in different and interesting ways.

3 **Are there any physical characteristics that need to be enhanced or minimized?**
Does your subject have great eyes, a big nose or wild hair? Are they tall, petite, skinny or chubby?

4 **How old is your subject?**
A setup for a baby can be arranged on a much smaller scale than an adult's.

5 **What does your subject want from the photo shoot?**
Men, including teenage boys, typically want to appear masculine and strong. Women, young and old, want to appear beautiful. Kids could care less how they look — they just want to have fun.

6 **Pre-visualize what YOU want from the photo shoot.**
Is there something about this subject that sparks an idea? How will you interpret this subject?

"You don't take a photograph, you make it."
– Ansel Adams

There's nothing like a real photo shoot to make you feel like a real photographer. Instead of just thinking like a photographer, you get to act like one, too. No matter how often you do it, the excitement is still there.

Before setting up your next photo shoot, take the time to consider the difference between **TAKING** a photograph and **MAKING** a photograph.

Anyone can TAKE a photo. Snap a picture from wherever you happen to be standing and — **click** — you've just taken a photo.

making a photo is

different. It's everything you've learned up to this point all rolled together. Making a photo isn't about stiff, posed images. In fact, the more you prepare in advance, the more spontaneous your photos will appear.

Look through our notes and steal some ideas for your own photo shoot.

PHOTOGRAPHER'S WORKBOOK

WHO: Ali and Lexi

PHYSICAL CHARACTERISTICS: Lexi is blonde, has beautiful skin and newly straightened teeth. Ali is brunette, has a contagious grin and charming freckles.

AGE: Both are 16-year-old high-school juniors.

RELATIONSHIP: Best friends, of course.

WHAT THEY WANT: A photo of themselves as friends. They also want to look pretty and sophisticated — sort of like supermodels.

PRE-VISUALIZE: Our goal is capturing the hip-and-trendy teenage vibe of these girls and their friendship.

Technical Decisions:

FIND THE LIGHT

Location — Living Room with three huge windows on west wall for lots of natural light.

CHOOSE THE FILM

Since it's about 3:30 pm and the windows are west facing, we have lots of light. 400-speed film will be fast enough.

WARDROBE

Let the girls know ahead of time to avoid busy stripes and textures, as well as excess jewelry.

EQUIPMENT

We'll use our 35mm to 135mm lenses to go wide and get in close.

The Setting

Bad Shirt

Good Shirt

journal entry: **Photo Shoot**

date: **March 6th**

Preparation/Setup:

1 Clear the space

2 Orient the setup to the light. We positioned our bench at a 90-degree angle to the windows.

3 Hang up a background. Low-tech masking tape works fine.

4 We placed a bench 4-6 feet in front of the backdrop. This will put the backdrop out of focus so it won't distract attention from the subjects.

5 **Modify the light** — With hard, direct light coming from two windows, we **BLOCKED** the top one with foam core and **DIFFUSED** the light coming in through the bottom. A **REFLECTOR** placed on the right side of our set evens out the light and ensures that both girls will be lit properly.

6 In this case, the photographer is parallel to the light source.

Hang Backdrop

Block the Top

Diffuse the Light

Place Reflector

Adjustments:

Ali's hair is so dark that she blended into the background, which made her look like a floating head. Good thing this wall (our new background) was a nice color.

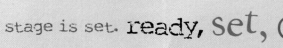
The stage is set. ready, set, click.

BURN SOME FILM

We used **three rolls** of film during this photo shoot. Out of all those pictures, we really only expect to get **one** that captures the moment magically. Most professional photographers average one to three usable shots per roll of 36 exposures. **DOESN'T THAT MAKE YOU FEEL GOOD?** It relieves the pressure of every frame having to be perfect. It also brings home the point that you have to break some eggs to make an omelet, so to speak. If you're only snapping a few exposures for each event or subject, you won't see the same success that you might if you were a little more generous with your film.

Straight On

High Camera Angle

DON'T JUST STAND THERE

Get Moving

— up onto a stool or ladder if needed. Down on your knees or even on your stomach. Whatever it takes to get the shot. This is all part of learning to see in a different way. If you shoot everything from a standing position, all your photos will start to look the same. Try getting up high or down low and you'll be amazed at the results.

PARTS

Is there an image within the image?
Move in closer and find out. Hands, feet, eyes, a sweet expression, even that little bit of skin above the belt.

GET OUT OF YOUR COMFORT ZONE

If you tend to shoot everything horizontally, try framing vertically (or vice versa). For a cutting-edge look, slightly angle your camera for a tilted frame that's neither horizontal nor vertical.

Angled Shot

SHOOT SOMETHING FOR YOURSELF

If a fabulous idea strikes you, shoot off a few frames for your own learning purposes. It's thebeginning of your portfolio.

ASK QUESTIONS

We always ask our subjects if there's anything in particular they'd like us to capture or any ideas they have about being photographed. This was the girls' favorite photo. It was their idea and they felt it captured their friendship the most.

BASIC PHOTO SHOOT GUIDELINES

(A.K.A. Disaster-Avoidance Strategies)

WHAT TO DO:

Exude confidence. Act like you know what you're doing and they'll think you do. **TAKE CONTROL** of the shoot fromthe beginning. Let kids and parents know what you expect. Talk to your subjects while photographing them. **Encourage them** and tell them how well they're doing. Give CLEAR directions. It's better to pantomime what you want them **TO DO** ather than just telling them.

- **HAVE CLEAN SNACKS** like Cheerios® on-hand for small children.

- **MUSIC** is a great relaxer. Ask teenagers to bring a favorite CD; have a couple of children's CDs on-hand to keep the kiddos in the mood for fun.

- **SQUEAKY TOYS** and puppets work well for getting children's attention. Use stickers on belly buttons and snap the baby trying to get it off.

- **RECRUIT AN ASSISTANT** — use parents if they won't interfere with the shot. We tell our parents before we start shooting that the only one allowed to direct the child is the photographer.

- **DRESS COMFORTABLY** because you're going to get a workout. It's amazing how physically exhausting a photo shoot can be. You're up, you're down, you're all around — doing anything it takes to get that perfect shot. If you have long hair, pull it up, wear your comfy clothes and have lots of water handy.

- **BACK UP** your equipment — make sure that you have plenty of batteries and film or digital media on hand.

After making every mistake in the book (and some that aren't listed yet), we've learned that what **NOT TO DO** is just as important as what **TO DO**.

WHAT NOT TO DO:

- **DON'T WAIT** until your subject arrives to start setting up. If you have everything ready to go ahead of time, you can spend your time being creative and having fun rather than fussing with technical details. Nobody wants to wait around while you get your act together (and babies and children won't).

- **DON'T FORCE** yourself to make too many decisions. Pick one background, one lighting setup, one film and one subject. Limit your variables.

- **DON'T TRY** to learn your camera during a shoot. Set your camera on auto exposure for this first shoot so you can get an idea of how well your auto program works with your film and lighting setup.

- **DON'T ALLOW** wardrobe changes for little kids. Whenever a mom walks in with a small child and five outfits, we know we're in

trouble. Before shecan get them out of the first outfit, the kid has had it. Choose your best set of clothes and go with it. We prefer naked babies any day, so clothing is optional in our studios.

- **DON'T TRY** a marathon session with small children. Keep it 15-20 minutes max.

- This is a biggie: **DON'T LET ANYONE** into the photo shoot that's not being photographed. If others are waiting their turn, have them wait in another room. If you're photographing multiple children, suggest that the parents bring a sitter to help manage.

- If someone wears glasses all the time, **DON'T MAKE** them remove them for the photo, even if they volunteer. Find a way to work around the glare (you can see if there's glare in the lens) or move the person until you don't see it anymore.

If you're shooting digitally, you can save time by just loading the images onto your computer, making notes and then re-shooting.

ASSIGNMENT

YOU WILL NEED:

- A three-hour block of uninterrupted time
- A well-behaved, willing subject
- A nearby one-hour photo processor
- One or two rolls of your choice film
- A backdrop (if desired)
- Stools or a bench (if desired)
- Post-It® Note Pads

1 Schedule a photo shoot during a time when you're completely undistracted by kids, phone, etc.

Give yourself at least 30 minutes to set up and 30-45 minutes to shoot.

2 Shoot at least one roll of film (36 exposures).

3 Try something you've never tried before. With that many exposures, you'll be unhappy with your results if you don't exercise creativity. Use some of our tips and make up some of your own.

4 Immediately take the film to your photo processor for developing.

5 Treat yourself — have lunch or our favorite, Diet Coke® and M&M's®, while waiting.

6 Pick up and evaluate your prints. Use the Post-It Notes to write down what went wrong or how you could have done anything differently (stick them on back of each photo).

7 Go back and immediately re-shoot again to apply what you've learned.

8 Repeat steps 4-6 (especially step 5).

8 Creative COMPOSITION

RULE OF THIRDS

Picture your frame segmented in thirds, both horizontally and vertically (like a tic-tac-toe board). If your subject is perfectly centered in the middle box, you might find yourself with a boring, static shot. To create more compelling pictures, place your subject on any of those imaginary lines — or even where they intersect.

When composing a portrait, it's a good idea to keep your subject's **head** (or in a close-up, **THE EYES**) on or near an **INTERSECTION** of these imaginary lines. If a person's eyes are at the halfway point, the forehead looks strange.

Great composition draws the observer into an image, turning a casual glance into a lingering gaze. Initially, composition is about being selective, making a decision about what to leave in and what to crop out of any given photo. Ultimately, composition is the ORGANIZATION of a **subject within an image**. It's the subtle layout of key elements that can make a merely good photo into something great.

Familiarizing yourself with some basic composition rules can help you to understand WHY you like a photo and — better yet — how to achieve similar results in your own work.

IN THIRDS

IN HALF

Nowhere is it written that a person's whole head has to be in the picture. Can you see how the rule of thirds is used here?

PARTY OF One

THINK VERTICAL

A common mistake for new photographers is taking every shot with the camera held horizontally, since that's what comes naturally. Most of the time, however, framing your subject vertically gives the best results. Since faces and bodies have a strong vertical axis, shooting vertically strengthens the image.

FACES

The most expressive part of a person is the face and within the face, the eyes have it. In other words, anything can be out of focus but the eyes.

WATCH IT!

Be careful not to crop pictures of people at their joints (elbows, wrists, waist, knees) or they might appear to be missing limbs.

THINK BALANCE

If you crop a subject tightly at the top of a picture, do the same at the bottom or your subject can appear to be floating out the top. At the same time, never crop tightly on bottom and leave too much space on top or a subject can appear to be falling out the bottom of the photo.

FULL LENGTH

When photographing a subject full length, remember to leave more space above the head than below the feet so your subject doesn't appear to be floating in space.

NOTE: Watch for the little reflections called "catch lights" to show up in your subject's eyes. Catch lights illuminate the eyes, making them appear alive and sparkling.

When photographing a standing person, it's essential to lower your camera to the subject's waist level. This allows your subject to look straight at the camera comfortably. It also eliminates distortions.

49

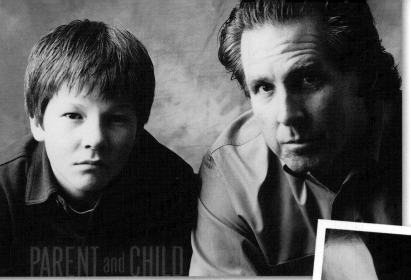

PARENT and CHILD

Pre-teen boys aren't likely to cuddle up with dad. Men and teenage boys generally like to maintain personal space when being photographed together.

friends

Girls and women are more often comfortable with sharing personal space. Have them tilt their heads slightly together to convey a sense of their closeness.

OR Two

Two people in a photograph gives your composition a **relationship** dynamic. In addition to each individual, the relationship becomes the photo's third subject.

The physical proximity of people in a picture speaks to their relationship. When asking people to sit or stand together, always respect their comfort zones. You can tell a lot by their body language and then respond to what seems to make them comfortable.

couples

Traditionally, men are photographed in an elevated, protective posture in relation to women. This works well, — but why not try something different? Photographing a couple on the same plane lends a more contemporary, informal feel to a photo…

R E L A T I O N S H I P S

Getting close to mom makes many children feel safe and comfortable in an unfamiliar situation. It also lets the photographer capture the bond between them.

OR More...

Arranging group photos can be the most challenging of all your photographic endeavors. Photographers tend to place their most significant subjects in the center and build out from there.

Set them up and let them interact rather than trying to achieve the perfect pose with everyone face-forward and smiling. If you prefer, start the traditional way. For example, get the Dad in place. But then secretly tell the boys to dog pile on top of him.

Ready, set — SHOOT!

BREAK SOME RULES

Conventional photographic wisdom advises against lining up a group of people for a photo. It's considered the "firing squad" method... But it all depends on HOW you position your subjects. In some scenarios, a line-up might be just the thing.

TRY LINING THEM UP AND LETTING THEM INTERACT

When grouping people, think in SHAPES. Triangles are particularly pleasing and easy to pose.

LINE THEM UP IN BIRTH ORDER

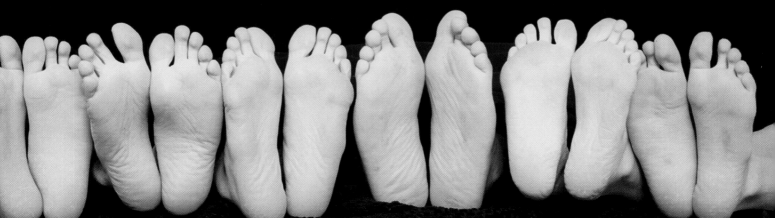

9 the BIG picture

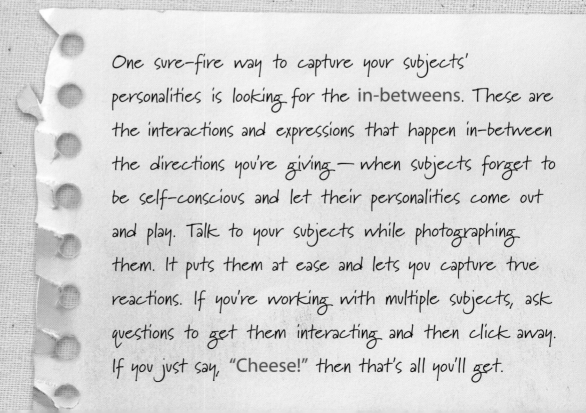

The big picture is about remembering why you're learning this stuff in the first place: so you can take beautiful photos; photos that say something, photos that interpret your subjects or capture their personalities like no one ever has before.

It's remembering that you need to really learn how your camera works, not to become everybody's favorite techno-wizard, but to **EXPRESS YOUR CREATIVE VISION,** your perspective.

The big picture is why you keep trying, again and again, when nothing's going right and your confidence is low. Because you know that at some point you'll get that shot. Then you'll know HOW you got it. And then there's NO STOPPING the great pictures you'll take.

"Success is what happens when 10,000 hours of preparation meet with one moment of opportunity."

– Anonymous

One sure-fire way to capture your subjects' personalities is looking for the in-betweens. These are the interactions and expressions that happen in-between the directions you're giving — when subjects forget to be self-conscious and let their personalities come out and play. Talk to your subjects while photographing them. It puts them at ease and lets you capture true reactions. If you're working with multiple subjects, ask questions to get them interacting and then click away. If you just say, "Cheese!" then that's all you'll get.

personality

"When I say I want
to photograph
someone, what
it really means
is that I'd like to
know them."

— Annie Leibovitz

Looking at the photos in this book, you'd think we spent our days in serene creativity, photographing calm, happy people and their well-behaved babies. **HONESTLY?** Nothing could be further from the truth. The truth is, most of these shots were taken amidst pure chaos. Babies crying and throwing up; toddlers (and some husbands) pouting, teenagers rolling their eyes and bossy mothers trying to run the show. We've seen it all.

persistence

patience

But through all this, we've learned that the **key to success IS KNOWING YOUR EQUIPMENT AND KEEPING YOUR COOL**. Never stop shooting. Watch for the in-betweens, those moments when the chaos clears. Though sometimes the chaos stays, and you can make that work for you, too. And still other times you have to know when to quit and try again another day.

It's hard work — we're always exhilarated and exhausted after a good photo shoot — excited about what we've captured and drained by what it took to get there.

We're going to go take a nap now...

NOTE: Take it easy when photographing your own children. We often put our own kids through more than we'd expect of any other child. Be kind and keep it fun for them.

"If I knew **HOW** to take a good photograph, I'd do it every time"

— Robert Doisneau

10 a MOMENT in time

Our lives are made up of moments, many of them seemingly insignificant in the overall scheme of things. It is those very moments that, woven together, **CREATE THE FABRIC OF OUR LIVES**. Often, we only think to capture big events or holidays. Capturing the moments between requires us to **see** the extraordinary in the ordinary. It requires the **SPIRIT** of a photojournalist.

There is a **truth** in photojournalism that isn't conveyed in mere snapshots. The subject appears unaware of the camera, the photographer becomes **A FLY ON THE WALL**, patiently waiting for just the right moment. Photojournalism is letting **LIFE** go on, not interfering at all with what's happening, just recording it as it happens. As the family photojournalist, you have access to those you love that no other photographer could possibly hope to have. The key is to keep your camera out and **USE IT**. After awhile, no one will pay attention to you anymore, you'll blend in — and get the **BEST PHOTOS** of your life.

These photos will become more precious over time as what **IS** becomes more and more removed from what **WAS**.

R E M E M B E R :

The only shots you regret are the ones you didn't take.

Start now.

A SAD STORY
My friend called me one day with a sad story. Her three sons were playing football in the backyard. They were actually having fun, not fighting or trying to kill each other. She had her hands in dishwater and called to her husband to get the camera. He rushed out back, camera in hand and yelled to the boys, **"Come over here boys and let me take your picture."**

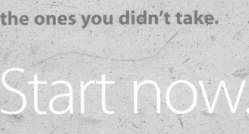

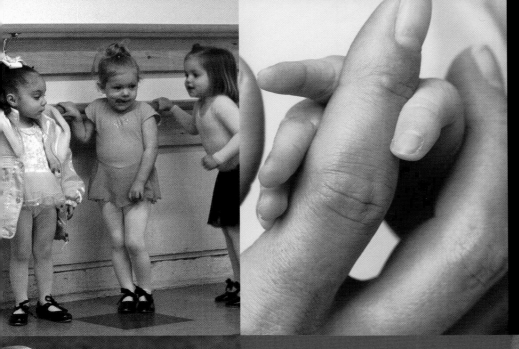

"…you can't help but wonder at just how sweet and sad and innocent all moments of life are rendered by the tripping of a camera's shutter, for at that point the future is still unknown and has yet to hurt us."

— Douglas Copeland

"Photography takes an instant out of time, altering life by holding it still."

— Dorothea Lange

I was wishing I could trade places with her, to take away her pain. I can't explain how proud I am of her, her attitude, her strength. Having this baby was like Christmas morning where everything comes alive.
— BRUCE, HUSBAND

I wanted to remember every detail of Zander eating a popsicle all by himself for the very first time. He was happily slurping away at it as it was melting faster than his little mouth was able to eat it.
— JANELLE, MOTHER

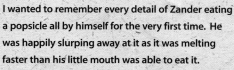

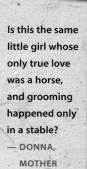

Is this the same little girl whose only true love was a horse, and grooming happened only in a stable?
— DONNA, MOTHER

The baby in this photo is now a long and lanky 11 year old boy. The chubby cheeks and dimpled hands are a thing of the past but that smile hasn't changed. He's still just as silly and happy as he was then. Still my baby boy.
— ALLISON, MOTHER

So similar in looks, yet so different in personality, my twins fascinate me. They have an uncanny ability to comfort each other, to read each other in all situations. It's an amazing connection. — IVAN, FATHER

My children don't think I know anything. My grandchildren KNOW I am the mistress of all knowledge. I mean, how do you compete with a woman who has endless band aids, a fridge stocked with treats and a purse full of change?

— KAREN, GRANDMA

A year before my mother died, I visited her home in Italy. One morning, when she thought I was still sleeping, she tiptoed into my room and carefully tucked the covers around me. No matter that I was a 74 year old man, a father and grandfather, I was still, always, her boy. — IVAN, SON

MAKE IT COUNT • CAPTURE LIFE'S DETAILS

You're never prepared for them to finally walk away. As hard as it was to let her go, my overwhelming feeling was one of deep happiness. Happiness for the person she was becoming; happiness for the love she had found and the life ahead.

— JERILYN, MOTHER

When I was a little boy, all I ever wanted to be was my Dad. He was always my hero and he still is. — DOUG, SON

intro to PHOTO ARTS

Developing your photographic skills will enable you to create images you can be proud of. Images that make the guy at the photo lab do a double take. Images that make your mom grab a hankie when she looks over the latest crop of grandkid photos. But a nice photo is far from the end of the road. **What are you going to do with that fantastic shot?**

Photo art is ART that has a photographic image as its foundation.

Great photos stand on their own. A clean, classic frame or portfolio is a perfectly legitimate way to showcase your work; galleries and museums have been doing it for centuries. But let that be your starting point, your springboard to the final photographic frontier — photo art.

Explore the possibilities of very tiny photos or the endless varieties of image-transfer techniques. You'll want to be hands-on with your photos once you see how many ways they can be used to create gifts and personalized celebrations of your life's events.

Join us as we enter a world where image is everything; your image, that is.

Discover the joy of manipulating photos into one-of-a-kind works of art through Polaroid transfers and mixed-media presentations. You'll find that working with images you have created is a powerful motivator to try something new; something a little wild, a little out there. **If photography alone hasn't gotten you in touch with your artistic side,** photo art will.

11 it's all in the presentation

Portfolios are artists' collections of their best work — and what better place to keep your finest work than a portfolio of your design? Your portfolio should reflect your personal vision and style. The following inspiring samples range from clean and classic to fresh and funky.

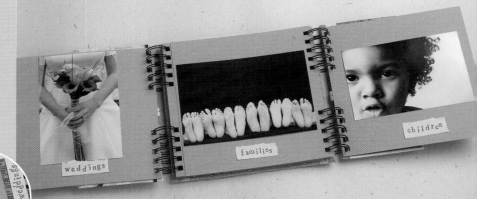

GATED PORTFOLIO
BY **JANELLE SMITH**
PHOTOS BY **JANELLE SMITH, DONNA**

THE PROCESS
A gated portfolio allows you to view three pages of your favorite photographs at once. This album has an unfinished cover, but you can use your favorite paper and doodads to decorate its "doors." Use some nice ribbon or twill tape for the perfect gate closure.

INSPIRE PORTFOLIO
BY **DONNA**
PHOTOS BY **DONNA**

THE PROCESS
This portfolio will accommodate prints up to 8" x 10". Start out by cutting two pieces of ph-neutral davey board into 10" x 12" pieces. Cut a 1" indentation in one of the boards to create a label tab. Use two pieces of printed twill tape 20" long. Measure the tape at 6" and sew in an elastic insert 2" long to accommodate portfolio expansion. Use grommets to secure the twill tape to the portfolio. Secure the latches to the cover and the twill tape as the closure. Embellish front of portfolio as you wish.

AMORÉ PROOF BOX
BY DEBBIE CROUSE
PHOTOS BY ALLISON

THE PROCESS

This sassy little box is the perfect place for keeping proofs from a favorite shoot. Remove all the pages from a book that's at least 4 1/2" x 6 1/2" (or slightly larger than the size of your proofs). Cover book with paper. Use chipboard to create a box that's slightly smaller than the book's dimensions (in this case, 4 1/8" x 5 1/8") allowing space for the bulk of several layers of paper cushioning. Score folds into the chipboard and reinforce box corners with book tape. Cover box. Glue bottom of box to inside back cover. Embellish with metal frames and a ribbon closure.

THE PROCESS

Start out with two sheets of 140-lb. 22" x 30" Hot Press Watercolor Paper. Using a cork-back metal ruler, measure and tear the paper into three sheets of 22" x 10". Fold in half for a finished size of 11" x 10". Tear a contrasting sheet of handmade paper in slightly larger dimensions for the cover. Slip a ribbon through the center of the folded pages and tie on the outside.

WATERCOLOR PAPER PORTFOLIO
BY ALLISON
PHOTOS BY ALLISON

Embossing Pages

Cut a piece of mat board to a size larger than the print you intend to display (i.e. 5" x 7" to accommodate a 4" x 6" print). Tape to the page with drafting tape. Press to a window or light box and score around the edge with a bone folder.

12 display dynamics

These whimsical display treatments bring entirely new levels of attention to your photos. Whether you're a flea-market fanatic or a staunch modernist, the following easy-to-make ideas are sure to delight.

CONTACT BABY
BY DONNA
PHOTOS BY DONNA

THE PROCESS
Have your local custom photo lab enlarge a contact sheet for you to frame (Donna's frame is 16" x 20" inches). Lay out consecutive negatives in a vertical, horizontal or mixed pattern. This treatment can be done with color or black-and-white negatives. The filmstrip numbers and holes create a contemporary homage to your baby.

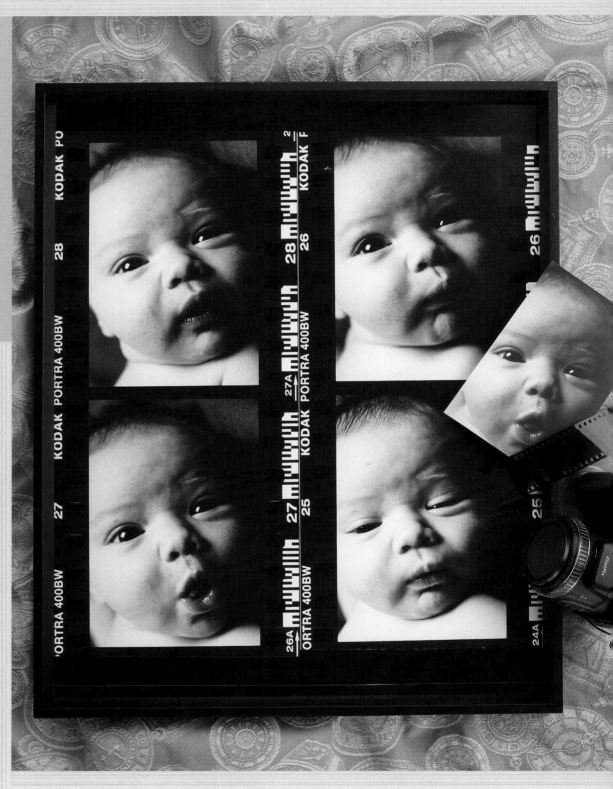

CLIPBOARD FRAMES
BY DEBBIE CROUSE
PHOTOS BY ALLISON, VINTAGE PHOTOS

THE PROCESS

Turn an ordinary little clipboard into an unexpected frame. Black frame: Mask off the silver clip and spray paint board. Rub on paste wax and then buff. Lightly rub with steel wool. Drill holes in the board for bolts (bolts should be 4-5" long), which create a support for glass and also a stand for the frame. Insert bolts through frame and secure in back with nuts. Attach label holder with small screws or long brads. For a cream-colored frame, spray paint over board and clip. Rub with steel wool the get a smooth finish. Sand in spots for a worn look. Rub and buff with furniture wax and brown shoe polish and lightly buff with steel wool. Attach bolts and label holder as shown.

THE PROCESS

Cut galvanized metal to desired size using tin snips. Cut an L-shape from the same metal to adhere to the back as a support stand. Bend metal piece and adhere to the back of the frame with superglue. Cut and bend two small U-shaped galvanized pieces for photo supports and superglue to the front of the frame. Use printed papers or acrylic paint for accents. You can also glue funky buttons to magnets to hold the photo onto the frame.

FUNKY FRAMES
BY DONNA
PHOTOS BY DONNA, JANELLE SMITH

display
and
framing

Use found objects and mementos to further tell the story your photos illustrate. Clip them to chicken wire or arrange them under glass for a charming tableau.

MY HERO
BY
DEBBIE CROUSE
PHOTOS BY
DONNA

THE PROCESS

To make a mini display special, put it under a glass dome. This not only protects items and keeps the dust away, it also gives a feeling of importance to a small grouping. Gather some of your favorite objects that belong to a specific person or family. The objects you collect will determine the size of dome you will need. Arrange in an interesting way with different levels, sizes, shapes and textures of objects to create an interesting still life.

THE PROCESS

Debbie had an 8" x 10" piece of rusty steel cut for her at a local metal shop. This covered the entire back of the shadow box. The photo was then attached to the plate with magnets. Assorted found objects were added to represent the tools and objects that these hands had worked with for so many years. The words were printed onto a transparency and placed next to the glass inside the frame. If possible, use your elements to display the photo, such as the bailing wire that holds up the smaller photo.

GRANDMA'S HOUSE STILL LIFE
BY DEBBIE CROUSE

The Postcard inside the dome reads:

Dear Granddaughter,

List of Enclosed Items—
Doorknob from Great-Grandma's house.
Photo of Emma with her brother Roy.
Salt Shaker from my collection.
Sample of my stitching handiwork.
And a piece of lace from my wedding dress.

I hope these items find you well.
All my love,
Grandmother Emma

ZANDER LOVES GRANDMA
BY JANELLE SMITH
PHOTOS BY JANELLE SMITH

THE PROCESS

This one's easy. Purchase a tray with a glass-framed bottom. Create a collage of your favorite photos with a note to Grandma. Include a drawing by her favorite grandchild and top it all off with painted prints of hands and tootsies.

COWLEY FAMILY

BY **DEBBIE CROUSE**

PHOTOS BY **ALLISON, DONNA**

THE PROCESS

Debbie started with a framed print at a garage sale. She loved the frame but hated the print. To recreate her work of art, start by replacing the print with chicken wire and stapling the wire to the back of frame. Then attach photos to the wire with assorted sizes of bulldog clips. Back buttons and "puddles" with push pins pushed from the front of the chicken wire into the torn corrugated cardboard on the back side of the wire. A veteran garage sale junkie, Debbie discovered uses for many of her vintage finds. A fold-up measuring stick frames the parent's photo, while a display ledge at the bottom of the frame (an old sewing machine drawer) encases a mini vignette using clever symbolism. A scrabble tile tray was used for spelling out the family name with letters from assorted games and typewriter keys. This family of 11 (nine children plus mom and dad) is represented in the flashcard 9 + 2 = 11. Notice that there are 11 tickets. Your finds too can add to your stories in subtle ways.

13 contact prints

Contact prints are index prints used by photographers for cataloging negatives. The name comes from the way contact prints are created: negatives are laid on photographic paper (making contact) and then exposed to light. Contact prints are largely utilitarian. But for us, contact prints are just one way we indulge our love of all things small. Little books, little photos — if it's little, we love it. Here are a few of our favorite little things to do with contact prints.

THE PROCESS

Cut up a contact print and place pieces on black cardstock. Using a white paint marker, write a journal entry on a piece of transparency film. Clip the transparency to the photo with a mini binder clip and adhere photo to the background page. Create the reset buttons using miniature blank dominoes edged and stamped with black Staz-On ink.

RESET BUTTON
BY ALLISON
PHOTOS BY DONNA

THE PROCESS

Make an accordion-fold book in a size that will fit a pendant frame. Attach contact-print-size photos and text to inner pages. Cut postcard/printed paper to fit cover and pages. Coat covers with Diamond Glaze. Drill tiny holes in bottom of frame. Attach charm and beads with fine wire through holes in frame.

MEMORY NECKLACES
BY DEBBIE CROUSE, DONNA
PHOTOS BY DONNA, VINTAGE PHOTOS

ON CONTACT
BY DEBBIE CROUSE
PHOTOS BY ALLISON

THE PROCESS
Choose a photo from a contact print. Create a background for your card by printing a list of phrases on cardstock. Cut the cardstock to size and fold in half. Turn up ends of card to create a pocket, both front and back. Then stitch sides of card. Slip wire photo holder onto the front of pocket. Add mini notes in pocket. Use one photo or a strip of photos and slip it into the other end of the wire photo holder.

CLAIRE
BY
ALLISON STRINE
PHOTOS BY
DONNA

THE PROCESS
Cut up a contact print from your photo shoot and use it to decorate yourscrapbook page. Mounting these mini photos onto clear film leader adds a photographic feel.

mini masterpieces

Soldered glass is the hottest trend going. Use it to create jewelry, ornaments and frames for your best photos — then give them as perfect little gifts. While the difficult-to-make appearance of soldered glass will certainly impress, it's actually quite simple to create.

THE PROCESS

Clean the glass to remove fingerprints and dust. Place photos onto glass with a small smudge of glue stick. Wrap exterior edges of the frame with copper foil tape and use the soldering method just to attach a chain. Paint the tape with a patina (follow manufacturers instructions). Let dry for 24 hours and retouch as necessary.

BALL AND CHAIN
BY **DONNA**
PHOTOS BY **DONNA**

SARAH
BY ALLISON STRINE
PHOTO BY DONNA

THE PROCESS

Use the soldering method to create glass-framed images. For extra depth, place a penny behind your photo (between the pieces of glass). To make the page background, stamp cardstock, then glue on cutout words. Paint the background with Lumiere Acrylic paints.

The Soldering Method

WHAT YOU NEED:
Thin pieces of glass (like in a picture frame)
Glasscutter and square
Copper foil tape
Bone folder
Lead-free silver solder
A soldering gun
Liquid flux
Paintbrush
Jump rings

Cut two pieces of glass for each item, using a glasscutter and square (or purchase pre-cut glass). Sandwich your image between the pieces of glass and carefully wrap the foil tape around the outside edges of the glass. Using a bone folder, burnish the tape firmly to the glass creating a tight seal. Paint liquid flux onto one section of the copper tape. Lay a bead of silver solder onto the same section of the tape using the soldering iron. Take one side at a time until the entire piece is soldered on all edges. Attach jump rings by painting a small bit of flux on the bottom of the jump ring and soldering to the finished piece.

CHARM BRACELET
BY DONNA
PHOTOS BY
DONNA, ALLISON

THE PROCESS
Working with tiny pieces of glass, use the soldering method to create charms. Attach charms and toggle clasp to a charm bracelet and use jump rings to complete the piece.

ORNAMENTS
BY ALLISON, JANELLE SMITH
PHOTOS BY ALLISON, JANELLE SMITH

THE PROCESS
Create your ornaments around any kind of photo prints. For an ornament with more texture, try printing your image on muslin and then fraying the edges for a softer look.

14 image transfer

An image transfer begins with a photo, but where it ends is anybody's guess. That fact that we can now transfer images to virtually any surface adds an entirely new dimension to photography. Produce your own stunning effects with the following techniques.

THE PROCESS
Print sepia-tone images onto inkjet fabric-transfer paper and then transfer to muslin following manufacturer's instructions.

LUKE
BY ALLISON STRINE
PHOTOS BY DONNA

GEL TRANSFER
BY CAROL WINGERT
PHOTOS BY
VINTAGE PHOTOS

THE PROCESS
Apply a coat of Liquitex Acrylic Matte Medium to a piece of natural cotton canvas. Set aside. Print a photograph onto regular copy paper. Paint Golden Gel Medium on face of photocopy and over the Matte Medium. Lay photocopy face down on fabric. Smooth with a brayer. Using the bottom of a spoon, burnish the paper firmly to the acrylic medium. Let it all dry overnight. When dry, lay fabric and paper in a shallow pan of water to dissolve the paper. Gently rub off paper to expose the transferred image.

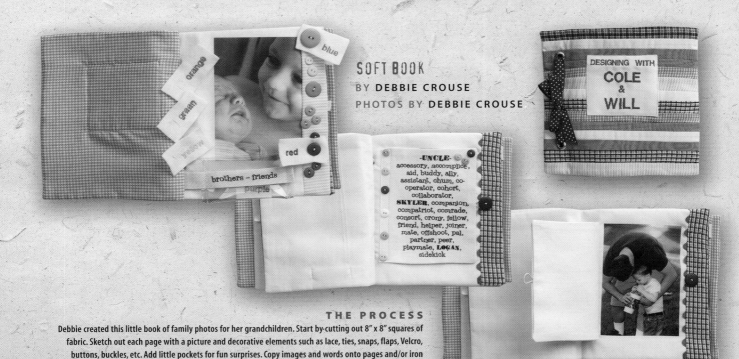

SOFT BOOK
BY DEBBIE CROUSE
PHOTOS BY DEBBIE CROUSE

THE PROCESS

Debbie created this little book of family photos for her grandchildren. Start by cutting out 8" x 8" squares of fabric. Sketch out each page with a picture and decorative elements such as lace, ties, snaps, flaps, Velcro, buttons, buckles, etc. Add little pockets for fun surprises. Copy images and words onto pages and/or iron transfers onto fabric as directed. To add body and sturdiness to the pages, use washable felt as interfacing. Attach grommets to each page, and then bind pages together with ribbon through grommets.

note

When transferring images, words and photos will transfer backwards. Make sure your images are backwards (in mirror mode) so that when transferred, they'll read correctly.

LEVI
BY DONNA
PHOTOS BY DONNA

THE PROCESS

Mix citrus solvent with water to the consistency of cream. Paint directly onto your printout. Lay watercolor paper on top of the painted image and burnish with a spoon or bone folder. Sew into an altered book.

packing-tape transfer method

Start with good-quality clear packing tape (e.g. Scotch® acid-free tape). Photocopy or print an image. Place a piece of packing tape onto the image and burnish using a bone folder or a spoon. Put the transfer into water and rub the paper off the tape backing until just a transparent image is left. After all that, the tape is still sticky enough to stay on the page.

BABY COLLAGE
BY DONNA
PHOTOS BY DONNA

THE PROCESS
Using a sturdy board or canvas as your base, first attach a dominant photo. Build a frame using crumpled, dyed glassine paper around the photo. Copy photos onto transparencies. Adhere transparencies with Diamond Glaze Adhesive. Use tape transfer method to for subtle baby faces. Finally, attach adornments.

blender-pen transfer method

Even if your images are black and white, photocopy them on a COLOR copier with carbon-based toner. This preserves the range of tones. Place the photocopy face down on the paper you are transferring it to and tape just one side of the copy to the paper with low-tack drafting tape. Using a xylene blender pen (e.g. Design Art), saturate the back of the photocopy with the pen. Burnish the image using a spoon or bone folder. Work in small sections, lifting the photocopy from time to time to check your progress. **IMPORTANT:** You must work in a well-ventilated area.

GIRLFRIENDS
BY ALLISON
PHOTOS BY ALLISON

THE PROCESS
Use the blender-pen transfer method to transfer images to cardstock. Tear and insert the cardstock into slits cut with an X-acto® blade into the backing cardstock. Use wire clips to attach a collage together, tucking other transfer all around the main image.

DANCE GIRLS
BY ALLISON STRINE
PHOTOS BY ALLISON

THE PROCESS
To make the tags, stamp ink and chalk onto shipping tags from an office supply store. For the image transfers, paint Gel Medium onto photocopies of the images. Then place a piece of silk material over the gel and burnish. Once dry, stitch image transfers to tags.

GRACE
BY CAROL WINGERT
PHOTOS BY DONNA

THE PROCESS
Enlarge a photo to approximately 5" x 7" on standard copy paper. Cut a piece of white or translucent shrink plastic slightly larger than the photo. Punch holes in all four corners. Lay the photocopy face down on shrink plastic. Use the blender-pen transfer method. Remove paper and shrink the plastic according to the manufacturer's instructions. When cooled, apply gold-leaf pen to edges. **Note:** Sometimes the paper actually becomes embedded in the plastic when the solvent "melts" the plastic. When heated, this gives the image added dimension.

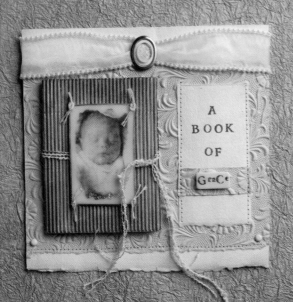

15 scanner art

The digital revolution has given us amazing new ways to be creative. You may already know the incredible things you can do with a flatbed scanner and a decent inkjet printer. Print photos onto glossy transparencies for a modern look or cardstock for an earthy appearance. Not equipped for high-tech output? Have someone else print your very own book for you.

LOYALTY AND DEVOTION
BY **CAROL WINGERT**
PHOTOS BY **ALLISON**

THE PROCESS
Scan photos and shrink so that multiple images fit on a page. Check your software's print drop-down for the multiple-print option, which will let you format photos for printing horizontally or vertically in rows. Select a layout to fit the size of your scrapbook page and print onto colored cardstock.

HALLOWEEN BOOK
BY **ALLISON** PHOTOS BY **ALLISON**

THE PROCESS
Upload a collection of digital images to a Web site that prints custom books (like www.kodak.com). In about a week you'll have your own hardcover book. The book you see here was designed in Apple iPhoto software on a Macintosh® computer.

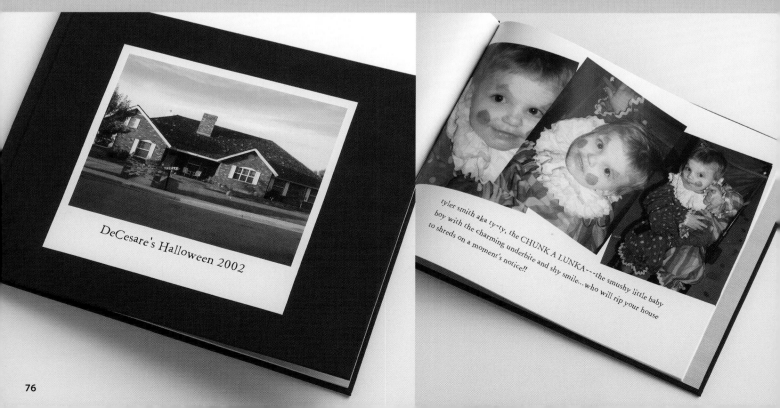

DeCesare's Halloween 2002

tyler smith aka ty-ty, the CHUNK A LUNKA---the smushy little baby boy with the charming underbite and shy smile...who will rip your house to shreds on a moment's notice!!

THE PROCESS

Using drafting tape, tape a piece of cardstock off into equal squares and paint with acrylic paint. Scan photos or import digital images into a design program using square boxes. Add text and print on transparencies. Mount trimmed transparencies into transparency holders backed with colored cardstock. Adhere completed transparency holders to page.

BEST FRIENDS
BY ALLISON
PHOTOS BY
ALLISON, DONNA

THE PROCESS

Work with a scanned photo or other digital image in an image-manipulation program (e.g. Adobe® Photoshop®). Change your picture's color or create a duotone. Print the photo onto colored cardstock. Use a cork-backed metal-edge ruler to tear straight edges. Layer the printout and cardstock. Use your scraps to create a little bundle that you can then tie with string and drip sealing wax onto for an old-world feel.

BABY LOVE
BY ALLISON
PHOTOS BY
ALLISON

JESSIE'S JOURNAL
BY DONNA PHOTOS BY DONNA

THE PROCESS

Color printing is done with four colors: cyan, magenta, yellow and black. Using a digital-imaging program like Adobe Photoshop, select one color channel at a time and print to give one-color digital images.

16 personalize it

Your pictures are little pieces of you. And nothing compares to the joy of sharing them in personalized ways. These artful ideas will help you celebrate family and friends any time. They'll be delighted to receive a beautiful baby picture suspended in a bar of soap, or just a simple note on family stationery. It's all about making the people you love feel special.

GRAD ANNOUNCEMENT
BY **DEBBIE CROUSE**
PHOTO BY **DONNA**

THE PROCESS
Print text onto vellum, then score and fold. Print inside text onto cardstock and then cut to fit vellum. Trim your photo and adhere to cardstock. Tie everything together in the fold with ribbon and attach charms. Finished card fits into a business-size (#10) envelope.

TINY FRAME CARDS
BY **DONNA**
PHOTOS BY **DONNA**

THE PROCESS
Cut up index prints and place underneath antique watch crystals. Adhere watch crystals to cards with Diamond Glaze.

WEDDING INVITATION

BY **ALLISON**

PHOTOS BY **ALLISON**

THE PROCESS

Arrange three images in boxes in a page-layout program. Print each image onto vellum separately, being careful to let each dry overnight. Print the invitation information on a backing card and place in a folder with ribbon closure. Create a personalized CD cover for love songs by printing images onto high-quality inkjet photo paper and trimming out.

THE PROCESS

Laser copy baby photos onto a transparency. Follow the instructions on mold for making your soap. Heat soap in microwave until melted. Let cool slightly and fill mold halfway. Drop transparency onto soap, being careful to get all air bubbles out underneath. Fill the mold the rest of the way (continue to beware of bubbles). When the soap is set, pop it out of the mold.

FAMILY STATIONERY

BY **DONNA** PHOTOS BY **DONNA**

THE PROCESS
Create your own family stationery using digital images in a page-layout program. Have a local copy shop print it for you — even in little personalized notepads (very charming). Make a stationery portfolio using chipboard and printed papers to keep it all organized.

cowley family stationery

17 polaroid transfer

Create something similar to an old fresco painting with a Polaroid transfer, a technique perfect for travel photos with timeless appeal. Then you have vivid Polaroid emulsion lifts, which can be transferred onto virtually any surface from a minimalist canvas to a thick piece of watercolor paper. Either method results in a completely unique work of art.

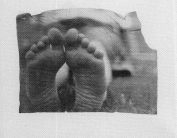

polaroid transfers

Transfer methods require Polaroid Polacolor 669 Film, which works in old Polaroid Land Cameras (check www.eBay.com or a camera shop) or in Daylab slide printers (details in product info section). The 669 film peels apart with both a positive and a negative side.

PARTS AND PIECES
BY **ALLISON**
PHOTOS BY **ALLISON**

THE PROCESS
Purchase ready-made stretched canvases at an art supply store. Using the Polaroid Emulsion Lift method, lay the emulsions directly onto the canvas. Let dry overnight and spray with a sealant.

POLAROID CARDS AND ART JOURNAL
BY **ALLISON, DONNA**
PHOTOS BY **ALLISON, JANELLE SMITH**

THE PROCESS
Use transfers or lifts for one-of-a-kind cards or entries in your art journal.

image transfers

Image transfers use only the negative portion of the film. You simply pull the print before the recommended developing time and press it onto a warm, wet piece of watercolor paper. After a few minutes, your transfer is complete.

emulsion lifts

Emulsion lifts use only the positive portion of the film (the actual photo). This method requires soaking the print in very hot water until the emulsion actually lifts off the print. Once the jelly-like emulsion is free, you can place it onto the wood, fabric, tile or paper of your choice.

OUR BEST ADVICE:
TAKE A WORKSHOP IN YOUR AREA
OR CHECK OUT WWW.POLAROID.COM
TO LEARN MORE.

THE PROCESS

Print a photograph or copy of a Polaroid transfer (at least 5" x 7" in size) two times onto a pebble-textured white cardstock. Cut one photo into horizontal 1" strips and the other photo into vertical 1" strips. "Weave" the strips together. The photo may be slightly "off" due to the papers being cut, but that adds to the artistic look created by this design. Lay the woven photo onto decorative paper and, using waxed linen and a sturdy needle, hand-stitch in place where the cut pieces meet. Adhere to decorative background paper.

PEACE AT HOME
BY CAROL WINGERT
POLAROID TRANSFER BY
JANELLE SMITH

PASSION PAGE
BY CAROL WINGERT
POLAROID TRANSFER BY
JANELLE SMITH

BARCELONA
BY CAROL WINGERT
POLAROID TRANSFER BY JANELLE SMITH

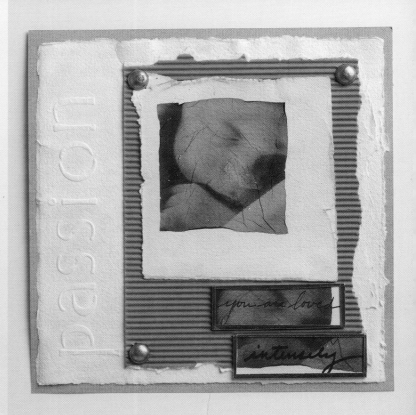

What exactly is "mixed media?" It's a little of this, a smidgen of that and a big dose of creativity. All together, it's a fascinating presentation of images. And you get to use each goody in your art supply bin to make it. Throw everything onto old postcards like Donna's Postcard Art or make a discreet little delight like Carol's Vintage Photo Box.

POSTCARD ART
BY DONNA
IMAGES BY DONNA

THE PROCESS
Select old postcards to embellish with all kinds of materials. Transfer images over your postcard collages with Lazertran transfer paper. Sew on a funky little pouch with pockets to keep postcards ready for sending special messages or simply displaying your artwork.

CONNOR
BY ALLISON STRINE
PHOTOS BY
DONNA, ALLISON

THE PROCESS
To create your background, use acrylic paint on canvas. Add Artist's Cement (by U.S. ArtQuest) and paint over. Photocopy an image onto Lazertran transfer paper. Roll out a thin sheet of Sculpey clay and place trimmed transfer onto the clay. Burnish the transfer and bake as directed. To make the nameplate, rub Vaseline onto each letter stamp and stamp onto copper. To age the copper, dip it into a solution of water and liver of sulphur.

THE PROCESS

Cover a CD tin with decorative paper. Print photos onto text-weight parchment paper. Cut and tear as desired and apply to tin face with other collage papers. Apply Anita's Fragile Crackle™ per manufacturer's instructions. When dry, brush on and quickly wipe off antiquing medium. Create a four-panel accordion-fold journal from handmade paper. Add cut or torn photos, decorative paper and embellishments. Paint the back of the tin. Attach the accordion to the inside of front and back covers and add embellishments to the cover.

VINTAGE PHOTO BOX
BY CAROL WINGERT
PHOTOS VINTAGE

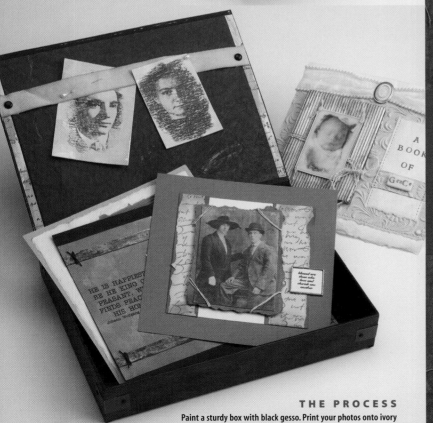

PHOTO JOURNAL ALTERED BOOK
BY CAROL WINGERT
PHOTOS BY CAROL AND VERN WINGERT

THE PROCESS

Print photos onto various papers such as cardstock, vellum, text-weight parchment, overhead transparency sheets and chipboard. Tear or cut photos and embellish pages with coordinating papers, charms, lace, buttons and metal accents. Cover the book with decorative papers and decoupage.

THE PROCESS

Paint a sturdy box with black gesso. Print your photos onto ivory cardstock. Cut or tear photos and add decorative paper to cover box top. Create decoupage with glossy Mod Podge® Apply Anita's Fragile Crackle per manufacturer's instructions. Antique with brown antiquing medium. Stipple ochre and brown Neopaque Acrylic paints onto the sides of the box. Add embellishments to the box's top and sides.

If you didn't want to try new things, you probably wouldn't be reading this book. This chapter in particular will challenge you to see your pictures in a different light. Doing so will give you the freedom to be brave with your work. Chop your images into a subtle wall hanging, or just snap a few extra frames of your favorite kiddo and develop an out-there collage with the results.

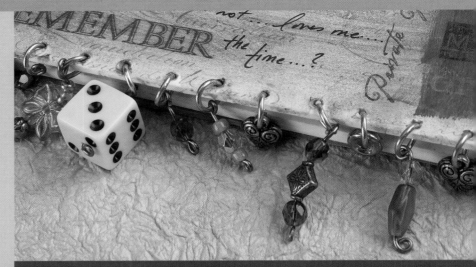

THE PROCESS

Start with an uncovered journal. Cut a square into the cover, which creates a frame for your photo inside. Using acrylic paints, inks and stamps, paint and distress the cover of the journal. Drill holes into the bottom of the journal with a tiny drill bit. Attach beads and embellishments using jump rings. Wrap silk and grosgrain ribbon along the edge and secure it with black nail heads.

ADORE JOURNAL
BY ALLISON
PHOTO BY
ALLISON

FRENCH BEDROOM
BY DONNA

THE PROCESS

Start with a 5" x 7" print and slice into approximately 1/2" strips. Glue onto handmade paper. Mount paper onto board for hanging and sew on ribbons and tassels for added decoration.

FAIRY BOTTLE
BY DONNA
PHOTOS BY DONNA

THE PROCESS

Use Lazertran to transfer an image onto a bottle. Add embellishments and smudges of acrylic paint. Top off with a wax-covered cork.

THE PROCESS

Take multiple photos of one subject in pieces, using your viewfinder as a grid reference. Assemble the separate photos into a whole by overlapping to match up the edges. Don't worry if they aren't perfect, it looks better that way. Use acrylic paints to create edge treatments on the page and staple details from other photos to scraps of cardstock.

JANIE BRAINY
BY ALLISON
PHOTOS BY ALLISON

A YEAR TO REMEMBER
BY DARIN DeCESARE
PHOTOS BY ALLISON, DARIN DeCESARE

THE PROCESS

Create a super-sized card with wood frames and hinges. Line the boxes with photos and sentiments recapping a memorable event or even an entire year in review. Add 3-D mbellishments for dimension.

20 leftovers

You'll always take more fantastic photos than you have room to display. That's what old shoeboxes are for, right? Not anymore. Here are some new solutions for sharing great photos that didn't quite make the frame. Scan them into a surrealistic vision of a vacation, like Steve's Parisian mélange or chop them up into a lively family journal. There are plenty of fresh ways to make the most of your leftovers.

FRENCH VACATION
BY STEPHEN SMYLIE

THE PROCESS
Using digital images of your vacation exploits, use photo-manipulation software like Adobe® Photoshop® to create a custom collage that embodies the spirit of your trip.

SLIDE JOURNAL
BY ALLISON
PHOTOS BY ALLISON

THE PROCESS
Cut up a sheet of slide preservers to accommodate the size of your journal or scrapbook page. Mount mini photos from a contact print into black slide mounts and place in the slide preserver. Using an awl, punch holes at every corner and tie to the journal with un-waxed linen thread. Use gaffer tape and Dymo labeling for added embellishments. Interior: Cut nine photos into approximately three-inch squares. Section off the first nine pages of a 10" x 10" spiral-bound album. Cut the pages using an Xacto knife and ruler, so that one square photo shows on each cut page. Use the extra space for journaling or embellishing.

Create a little quilt of photos by zigzag stitching picture pieces together onto a text-weight paper background. Add in words if you like. Adhere your quilt to the front of a journal. Affix a metal plate on top of your collage using an awl to make the holes and long brads to hold the plate in place. Using magnets, stick a title and some ephemera from the trip to the metal plate. Keep the journal closed with a funky rubber band.

MAGNET TRAVEL JOURNAL
BY ALLISON
PHOTOS BY ALLISON

THE PROCESS

MAD'S DOG ACCORDION BOOK
BY **ALLISON S.**
PHOTOS BY **DONNA S.**

THE PROCESS
Add Artist's Cement (U. S. Artquest) to your cover. When it dries, paint over it with Lumiere Acrylic Paints. Then go nuts: add any kind of embellishment that feels right.

freezer-paper method

Cut a piece of muslin to 8.5" x 11" (or whatever size your printer requires). Iron the muslin to the waxy side of a piece of freezer paper. This stabilizes the muslin and lets it feed through the printer. After printing, iron the printed muslin to heat-set the ink. Print words, images or whatever strikes your fancy. This method also works well for bits and pieces of fabric.

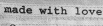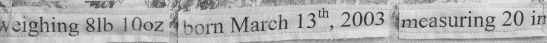

GRACE QUILT
BY DONNA
PHOTOS BY DONNA

THE PROCESS
Cut leftover photos into equal squares and zigzag together on with a sewing machine. Print assorted words onto muslin using the Freezer-Paper Method and sew muslin borders between the photos. Attach rings to complete.

Artist Bios

Allison Tyler Jones

Allison is the founder and co-owner of Memory Lane Photo and Paper Arts in Mesa, Arizona. Allison has written for Creating Keepsakes Magazine and Publications International. She teaches workshops on art journaling and photography at the store. Her interests include photography, writing, reading and journaling.

Allison lives in Mesa, Arizona with her totally hot husband, Ivan. She is the mother of two and stepmom to five talented and wild kids. She is the oldest sister of a huge family and counts her relationships with family and friends as the greatest gifts life has to offer.

TEAMWORK

Donna Smylie

Australian-born Donna is co-owner of Memory Lane Photo and Paper Arts. She spends her days working at the store and her nights designing for 7gypsies, which she owns with her sexy Irish husband, Steve. She is the mother of seven children and one very new granddaughter.

Donna earned her bachelor's of science from Brigham Young University. She has taught Special Education in Australia, Utah and Arizona. However, nowadays she teaches workshops in soldering, book arts and photography.

Her interests include travel and spending time with her family. She is grateful to her parents, her husband and children for all their inspiration, love and encouragement.

Debbie Crouse

Debbie has worked for Memory Lane in Gilbert, AZ for four years. She is a veteran contributor to all the Autumn Leaves books: *Designing with Vellum*, *Designing with Notions* and *Designing with Texture*. When she's not working on books or designing displays for the store, she is busy designing product for 7gypsies. She lives in Mesa, Arizona with her wonderful husband Skip. They have four children and two gorgeous grandchildren.

Allison Strine

Allison Strine is an artist who has been featured in Creating Keepsakes' *Scrapbooking With Style* and many other publications. She is a Creating Keepsakes Hall of Famer 2002. She lives in Atlanta, GA with her husband Lloyd and her children Olivia and Ethan.

Carol Wingert

Carol teaches book arts and scrapbooking workshops at Memory Lane. She has been published in Legacy and Creating Keepsakes Magazines and has just completed work on a book for Design Originals. Carol lives in Gilbert, Arizona with her sweet and supportive husband Vern and their daughter Ashley.

Janelle Smith

Janelle, a former Memory Lane photo student, is currently pursuing a fine arts degree in photography at the University of Utah. She lives in Salt Lake City with her husband and biggest fan Zach, their two-year-old son Zander and rotweiller Wesley. She is opening her own photo studio, *Atelier Photographie*, and will be graduating this summer.

CREATIVITY

OTHER CONTRIBUTORS:

Darin DeCesare

Darin owns a graphic design firm, is a supreme golfer and former state racquetball champion. He lives in Mesa, Arizona with his wife Caroline.

Steve Smylie

Steve is the creative genius behind the 7gypsies line. He is also a former architect and art teacher. He lives in Mesa, Arizona with his wife Donna and their children.

A NOTE OF THANKS:

We'd also like to thank Steve Scarlett and Jeff Larson for providing us with "before" photos so incredibly bad that they made us look good. Thanks guys!

CREDITS

Photo Credits

All photos in this book by Allison Tyler Jones or Donna Smylie except where indicated. All product and project photography by Dave Tevis of Tevis Photographic, Tempe, AZ.

TITLE PAGE
Boys on Left: by Carol Harris
Little Girl on Right: by Ruth Giauque

DEDICATION PAGE
Top Left in Vertical Strip:
Boy by Mel Gudmundsen,
Young Girl by April Dominguez,
Newborn by Miriam Hahn,
Baby by Shannon Jones
Senior on Left: by Melissa Harper
Little Boy Middle Left:
by Ruth Giauque

CHAPTERS 1–10
PAGE 8
Before Sharon by Steve Scarlett
PAGE 11
Grandma and Grandson
by Ashley Whiting
PAGE 12
Little Girl by Crystal Folgmann
PAGE 20
Girls Dancing by Crystal Folgmann
PAGE 21
Father and Daughter
on Beach by Pamela Allison
Basketball Shot by Unknown
PAGE 22
Indian Princess by Miriam Hahn
PAGE 22-23
Brothers in Color/BW
by Debbie Crouse
PAGE 30
Girl on Bike by Steve Scarlett
PAGE 32
All Photos by Janelle Smith

PAGE 34
Vertical Baby Photo
by Janelle Smith
PAGE 39
Dad and Baby in Collaboration
with Elizabeth Opalenik
PAGE 41
Grandmother by Ashley Whiting
PAGE 54
Baby and Aunts by Janelle Smith
PAGE 56
Breakfast Boy by Sharon Scarlett
and Sad Tale Photo by Jeff Larson
PAGE 57
Silhouette Baby in Window
by Janelle Smith
PAGE 58
Baby Eating Popsicle
by Janelle Smith

Product Credits

Products without a credit are either part of the artist's personal stash or not available for purchase.

CHAPTER 11
IT'S ALL IN THE PRESENTATION
PAGES 62-63

GATED PORTFOLIO
GATED JOURNAL: 7gypsies
STUDS/EMBELLISHMENTS:
7gypsies
PRINTED PAPER: 7gypsies, EK
Success and Emaginations
RIBBON: Memory Lane
STAMPS: Personal Stamp Exchange

INSPIRE PORTFOLIO
ART BOARD: 7gypsies
TWILL TAPE: 7gypsies
FASTENERS: 7gypsies

STAMPS: Turtle Press Studios
PAINT: Neopaque Acrylics

AMORE PROOF BOX
EMBELLISHMENTS/FRAMES:
Becky Nunn Designs
PAPERS: 7gypsies and The Paper Co.
RIBBON: Mokuba Ribbon

WATERCOLOR PORTFOLIO
PAPER: Savoir Faire
RIBBON: Memory Lane

CHAPTER 12
DISPLAY DYNAMICS
PAGES 64-67

CONTACT BABY
FRAME: Aaron Bros.

CLIPBOARD FRAMES
CLIPBOARDS: Office Max
BOLTS: Home Depot
LABEL HOLDERS: Anima Designs
PAPER: 7gypsies and K & Co.

FUNKY FRAMES
PAPERS: 7gypsies
METAL/HARDWARE: Home Depot

MY HERO
SHADOW BOX: Aaron Bros.

ZANDER LOVES GRANDMA
TRAY: Michael's Crafts

GRANDMA'S HOUSE STILL LIFE
DOME: Tuesday Morning

CHAPTER 13
CONTACT PRINTS
PAGES 68-71
MEMORY NECKLACES
PENDANT FRAMES: 7gypsies

ON CONTACT
WIRE PHOTO HOLDER: 7gypsies
CARDSTOCK: National Cardstock

CLAIRE
LEATHER PAPER: Emaginations
OTHER PAPER: Forget Me
Not Papers

BALL AND CHAIN
SOLDERING SUPPLIES:
Grainger Hardware

CHAPTER 14
IMAGE TRANSFER
PAGES 72-75

SOFT BOOK
TRANSFER PAPER: June Tailor
BUTTONS: Hill Creek Designs
TWILL TAPE AND RINGS: 7gypsies

BLESSINGS
STAMP: Stamp in the Hand
FRAME: Becky Nunn Designs
CARDSTOCK: National Cardstock

LEVI
TWILL TAPE: 7gypsies

DANCE GIRLS
PAPER: Magenta
FIBERS: Rub A Dub Dub

GIRLFRIENDS
PAPER: K & Co.
RIBBON: Mokuba Ribbon
WIRE SPIRALS: 7gypsies
SECRETS BRASS PLAQUE:
Memory Lane
STAMPS: Stampers Anonymous
and Hero Arts
CARDSTOCK: National Cardstock

GRACE
PAPER: Solum World Paper
SHRINK PLASTIC: Lucky Squirrel

FIBERS: On The Surface
DOMINO: Memory Lane
STAMPS: Personal Stamp
Exchange
RIBBON: Memory Lane

CHAPTER 15
SCANNER ART
PAGES 76-77

BEST FRIENDS
TRANSPARENCY HOLDERS:
Memory Lane

BABY LOVE
JOURNAL: Magenta
GOLD LEAFING: Amy's Gold Leaf
LABEL FRAME: Becky Nunn Designs
PAPER: Anna Griffin

LOYALTY AND DEVOTION
METAL FRAME: Making Memories

JESSIE JOURNAL
JOURNAL: 7gypsies

CHAPTER 16
PERSONALIZE IT
PAGES 78-79

COWLEY STATIONERY
PAPER: Chatterbox Inc.
PHOTO CORNERS:
Becky Nunn Designs
HINGES/CLOSURE: Darice Inc.
MINI FRAME: 7gypsies
ENVELOPES: Memory Lane

CHAPTER 17
POLAROID TRANSFER
PAGES 80-81
PARTS & PIECES
READY MADE CANVAS:
Flax Art Supplies

BARCELONA
WAXED LINEN: 7gypsies
WALNUT INK: 7gypsies
STAMPS: Green Pepper Press

PEACE AT HOME
COPPER STRIPS: Amaco
PATINA: Chemtek

PASSION
GLASS SLIDES: Memory Lane
COPPER TAPE: Memory Lane
STENCILS: Wordsworth
PAINT: Jacquard Acrylics
NAILHEADS: 7gypsies

CHAPTER 18
MIXED MEDIA
PAGES 82-83

CAROL'S BOOK
Tape Measure & Lace Page
PAPER: 7 gypsies
LACE/BUTTONS: Joanne's Fabrics
STAMPS: Judi-Kins
ANTIQUE BRADS: American Tag

MOVING DAY PAGE
STAMPS: Green Pepper Press;
Stampers Anonymous
INK: Brilliance and Staz-on by
Tsukineko
COPPER: Amaco

POSTCARD ART
PRINTED TWILL: 7gypsies
MINI FRAMES: 7gypsies

PHOTO TIN
PAPER: 7gypsies, Penny Black
STICKER: Stampendous
PAGE PEBBLES: Making Memories
CLOCK CHARM/NAILHEADS:
7gypsies
MESH: Magenta
PAINT: Jacquard Lumiere

CHARMS: Designs By Pamela
LABEL HOLDER: Anima Designs
BRADS: American Tag
CRACKLE: Anita's Fragile
Crackle-Duncan
FINISH: Antiquing Medium-Plaid

VINTAGE PHOTO BOX
PAPER: 7gypsies
METAL LEAVES:
Becky Nunn Designs
PEWTER LETTER TILES:
Global Solutions
FERN PUNCH: The Punch Bunch
BLACK NAILHEADS: 7gypsies
WALNUT INK: 7 gypsies

CHAPTER 19
OUT THERE
PAGES 84-85

A YEAR TO REMEMBER
HINGES: Home Depot
LUMBER: Home Depot
FABRIC: Joanne's Fabrics

FRENCH BEDROOM
GOLD SPINES: 7gypsies
RIBBON: Midori

JANIE BRAINY
PAINTS: Jacquard Light Acrylic

ADORE JOURNAL
JOURNAL: 7gypsies Naked Journal
NAILHEAD/HARDWARE:
7gypsies Hardware
BEADS: Designs by Pamela

CHAPTER 20
LEFTOVERS
PAGES 86-89

MAGNET TRAVEL JOURNAL
JOURNAL: 7gypsies
MAGNETIC NAMEPLATE: 7gypsies
PAPER: 7gypsies

SLIDE JOURNAL
SLIDE HOLDERS: Savage
JOURNAL: 7gypsies
LINEN THREAD: Hill Creek Designs
SLIDE MOUNTS: Memory Lane

MAD'S DOG BOOK
ACCORDION BOOK: 7gypsies
STAMPS: Wordsworth

GRACE QUILT
MUSLIN/FABRIC: Joanne's Fabrics
PRINTED TWILL: 7gypsies
TRANSFER PAPER: June Tailor
RINGS: 7gypsies

Thanks to the following companies who supported our efforts:

7GYPSIES
www.7gypsies.com
480-325-3358

BECKY NUNN DESIGNS

MEMORY LANE PHOTO AND PAPER ARTS
1275 E. Baseline Rd #104
Gilbert, AZ 85233
480-844-9004
www.memorylanearizona.com

About Us

Autumn Leaves

A full line of papers, vellums, books, and stickers, and adding exciting new categories each year!

Autumn Leaves began in the stationery industry six years ago. At one point, we noticed that paper sales were increasing at a far greater pace than envelope sales. After a time, we realized that our papers were being purchased by scrapbookers who, of course, didn't need envelopes; just beautiful papers.

'Lo and behold, a new company was born!

Soon after, Autumn Leaves began making stickers and vellum pages, becoming well known for layered, lush vellums and the acquisition of the popular Whispers line of photographic vellums.

Realizing the need for an idea book about vellum, Autumn Leaves published Robin Johnson's *Designing With Vellum* in September, 2001. Released under the imprint *"The Sophisticated Scrapbook,"* it is now in its third printing.

Designing with Notions was the second big book in the series, followed by the tremendously popular *Designing with Texture*, where the Autumn Leaves team found some of the most unique surfaces in imaginable.

Now we bring you *Designing with Photos*, a truly all-in-one guide to photographing like a professional, and using your photos in incredibly artistic ways. Presented by Memory Lane founders Allison Tyler Jones and Donna Smylie, who literally led the Arizona school where all the great Autumn Leaves'artists got their start.

Autumn Leaves plans to continue with papers, vellums, stickers, and idea books, as well as the terrifically exciting Seven Gypsies. Watch for new product releases throughout the year as the company grows, and the forward thinking continues.

Stickers

America's Fastest Growing Cardstock Company

collections from the journey

Autumn Leaves
4917 Genesta St.
Encino, CA. 91316

For Information,
Contact:

Josie Kinnear [Operations Manager]
Tim Collins .... [Marketing Director]

Vellums

Papers

Journals

Papers

Long Distance
1.800.588.6707

Local
1.818.907.5977

Fax
1.818.380.6776

To Contact National Cardstock Please Call:
P. 1.866.452.7120 | F. 1.866.452.7121

"Which of my
photographs is
my FAVORITE?
The one I'm
going to take
tomorrow..."

—Imogen Cunningham